Dear Baby

Our Angel We Lost, Love and Honor Forever

Tani Leeper
with John Leeper

First published by Ultimate World Publishing 2020
Copyright © 2020 Tani Leeper and John Leeper

ISBN

Paperback: 978-1-922372-98-7
Ebook: 978-1-922372-99-4

Tani Leeper and John Leeper have asserted their rights under the Copyright, Designs and Patents Act 1988 to be identified as the authors of this work. The information in this book is based on the authors' experiences and opinions. The publisher specifically disclaims responsibility for any adverse consequences, which may result from use of the information contained herein. Permission to use information has been sought by the authors. Any breaches will be rectified in further editions of the book.

All rights reserved. No part of this publication may be reproduced, stored in or introduced into a retrieval system, or transmitted in any form, or by any means (electronic, mechanical, photocopying, recording or otherwise) without the prior written permission of the authors. Any person who does any unauthorized act in relation to this publication may be liable to criminal prosecution and civil claims for damages. Inquiries should be made through the publisher.

Cover design: Ultimate World Publishing
Layout and typesetting: Ultimate World Publishing
Editor: Hayley Ward

Ultimate World Publishing
Diamond Creek,
Victoria Australia 3089
www.writeabook.com.au

Testimonials

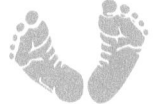

"I have spent the last 30 years as a physician serving infertile couples. I have walked alongside my patients as they have experienced the elation of pregnancy, and as they have experienced the devastation of treatment failure and pregnancy loss. By far the greatest emotional trauma has been associated with pregnancy loss. Nothing is more devastating than the initial celebration of pregnancy, of a dream realized, only to be unexpectedly and abruptly torn away. Compounding this devastation has been the lack of resources to support couples and guide them through their grief. In Tani and John Leeper's book, *Dear Baby*, we now have a superb resource to fill this void. Their knowledge, experience, and wisdom combine to form the perfect blend of information, understanding, empathy, and compassion, along with the vital ingredients of future possibility and hope. I highly recommend *Dear Baby, Our Angel We Lost, Love and Honor Forever.*"

Jeffrey Nelson, D.O.
Fellow of the ACOOG HRC Fertility

"If you have experienced or perhaps are currently experiencing perinatal bereavement, each word within this must-read book—this work of love—will touch your heart and soothe your soul, while serving as a testament that you are not alone in your loss.

Told through the lens of both mom and dad, Tani and John Leeper provide deeper insights and profound revelations into the indelible mark each pregnancy loss leaves. Their transformative experiences help us to discover how true unconditional love and the ethereal are both interconnected. An interconnectedness that when realized, guides us to a place of boundless spiritual growth.

Having personally experienced several miscarriages, including a midterm miscarriage of twins several years ago, I found this book emotionally invaluable as it drew me into a much-needed cathartic and spiritually uplifting state of being.

Dear Baby is a book of triumph and inspiration; transforming tragedy and despair into hope and a greater sense of spiritual love."

Amber Rose Washington
Author, Songwriter, Public Speaker

"Whether you've personally gone through a pregnancy loss or have walked alongside a family member or friend who has suffered such a loss, you will find hope and healing in reading *Dear Baby, Our Angel We Lost, Love and Honor Forever*.

Tani and John Leeper's book fills the gap as a testimony of the journey from the darkness of losing a precious child to the light of understanding and peace.

The reality of pregnancy loss affects so many families each year. The true path to hope and healing is now revealed in Tani and John's, *Dear Baby, Our Angel We Lost, Love and Honor Forever*. It stands unique as a vital resource which I am honored to highly recommend."

Michael North
Worship Pastor, Shepherd Church,
Los Angeles, CA

"*Dear Baby* is such a wonderful and inspiring book for any parent or family member who has suffered through the loss of an unborn child. Reading both John and Tani's thoughts and feelings about their story, I was able to feel a connection with them and their babies that they lost. Not only is this such a beautiful story from both parents, it's a book that will help you to understand that you are not alone and there are groups out there to support you. Thank you, John and Tani, for sharing this lovely, angelic story with the world."

Christine Rizzo
Author, Certified Life Coach

"Many are afraid to talk about the negative effects of pregnancy loss, miscarriage, stillbirth, or the like. The inexplicable and complex pain that Tani and John's babies left became the anchor of their mission, and gave birth to a new meaning. *Dear Baby* is a book that will become a companion to those who experience the same tumultuous storm that only few ever dare to speak of, yet speaking is exactly what Tani and John did.

Dear Baby will bring a mixture of emotions to everyone who suffered the same fate…pain, joy, hope, faith, and above all, love. Love that travels beyond this time…our babies that have never been forgotten. Sharing their story is needed to understand that we are never alone in any battle."

Mari & Raymond Orosa
LifeGroup Members, Shepherd Church,
Los Angeles, CA

"Many things can be said when someone loses a child, but all too often, they can be clichés. In their memoir, *Dear Baby*, Tani and John offer their readers everything but stereotypes. After reading the painstaking documentation of the horrific events in their lives, I walked away with hope. Their insight into the interworkings of a broken heart puts the reader at ease with a better understanding of perspective and hope. Their level of compassion and empathy drips off the pages. As parents and followers of Jesus, they offer us all lessons on faith and fortitude. I recommend this book to parents who have faced the burden of losing a child or those looking to better understand a loving God who allows it to happen."

Abe Anaya
LifeGroup Pastor, Shepherd Church,
Los Angeles, CA

"Tani and John are a great example of God's faithfulness. To endure what they went through and still have the heart to help others, speaks volumes. I know their story, but reading *Dear Baby* makes me emotional as if I'm hearing it for the first time. This book will touch you."

Kat Devera
Angel Mom to Michael Dexter

"*Dear Baby* will help men gain an understanding as to what their partner is going through, and vice versa. John and Tani candidly share their emotions about loss, making you realize you are not alone in this struggle. If you have walked, or are currently walking, on a similar path, you will quickly realize you share many of the same emotions of anger and pain. And through it all, learn to appreciate that God is always there for you."

Kenny Bernas
Angel Dad to five angel babies

"Losing a child poses so many questions, coupled with pain and hurt. It's not talked about much, therefore making you feel alone. It would have been nice to be handed a manual on how to grieve and how to heal. This is what *Dear Baby* has done. It truly walks you through dealing with loss, understanding it, and getting to a place of healing, and even celebration. For that, I am forever grateful! Reading this book will bring you hope and peace."

Valerie Alviar
Angel Mom to Gabriel Joseph

"*Dear Baby* shines a much-needed light on a topic that is often left to sit in the dark. Tani and John's story brings hope and validation to those who have experienced the tragedy of child loss. And even more, it brings understanding and insight to those who walk alongside angel moms and dads."

Richard Inez
Angel Dad to Vinny

"Going to therapy after losing my son when he was only five days old still left me hopeless and empty. It wasn't until I heard other moms' and dads' stories of loss that I found hope again. This is what John and Tani have done in this must-read book on grief and survival. They bravely share their story and give parents of loss a place to share theirs. Our losses are different, yet we share the same grief. *Dear Baby* will take you out of the darkness of feeling you are the only one."

Raquel Rivera
Angel Mom to Ayden Johnny

"*Dear Baby, Our Angel We Lost, Love and Honor Forever* is a beautiful journey lovingly shared by Tani and John Leeper. Their personal story is intended to open a conversation of the lonely struggle of an unbearable loss, to finding hope and healing through faith, support, and community.

Most often it is the mother's voice heard in her pain of miscarriage, stillbirth, or neonatal loss, but *Dear Baby* offers a unique and much-needed view from a father's perspective of losing a child. In addition, the beautiful compilation of achingly honest letters from angel mothers, fathers, siblings, and grandparents bring about an immense comfort and reassurance that you truly are not alone in your personal journey.

This valuable resource will continue to bring awareness to pregnancy and infant loss and encourage you to continue to love and honor your angel forever. I am beyond honored to highly recommend this amazing piece of work as a labor of love for all our angels gone too soon."

Gladys P. Jabonillo
Angel Mom to Xavier Gregory

Dedication

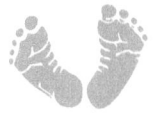

Dedicated to all the babies gone too soon; this is your legacy. Your stories will bring comfort to the broken-hearted.

Contents

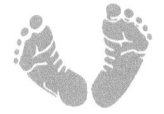

Testimonials	iii
Dedication	xi
Foreword	xv
Introduction	xix
CHAPTER ONE: It Shouldn't Be This Hard	1
CHAPTER TWO: The Unimaginable Reality	17
CHAPTER THREE: My Ethereal Love	35
CHAPTER FOUR: The First Cut is the Deepest	47
CHAPTER FIVE: The Ultimate Test of Faith	61
CHAPTER SIX: Love, Honor, and Cherish…Always	73
CHAPTER SEVEN: Dear Baby	87
About The Authors	145
Acknowledgements	151
Speakers	155

Foreword

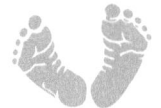

"I'm so sorry for your loss." After my miscarriage, these words were not comforting. They implied that my child was gone, and sadness was the only emotion to be felt. I just couldn't accept that. Though part of my world for only a brief time, my baby impacted my heart greatly. So why would God give me the amazing gift of a child, only to take it back? With a legitimate question for God, there is really only one place I could look for His answer—in the Bible. In Jeremiah 1:5, I read:

> *"Before I formed you in the womb, I knew you,*
> *before you were born, I set you apart."*

So, not only does God intentionally form life in a mother's womb, but He also has a purpose and a plan for that life—not at birth—but clearly before? Oh, the peace and hope that washed over me as I read these words, God's words.

For if God knew Jeremiah this way, He knows all He creates in the same way. My baby, your baby, every baby.

At that moment, I was ready to dedicate the rest of my life to finding my baby's purpose. I now had proof that he had one, I just hoped I would learn it on this side of eternity. In time, I began to think of the hundreds and thousands of devastated moms like me, who were hurting and could possibly begin to heal as I did, by learning this truth.

In 2013, nearly a year-to-date after my own miscarriage, I started a support group with the blessing of my church as its host. It was to be a place for hurting moms to gather weekly, seeking a space to share the love they felt for a baby that the world seemed to already forget.

The only thing is...dads showed up too! While this was not the reality of my own life, I was encouraged to see a circle full of couples amongst the tissue boxes ready to reveal a pain that nobody wanted to talk about. One of those couples was John and Tani Leeper.

They came to the group in a state of shock, fresh from their loss and desperate for a glimmer of hope. They wasted no time in challenging me, but each week I grew to appreciate their honesty and vulnerability. Tani was bold in her questioning to why this had happened to them. John, despite his own pain, just wanted to comfort his wife. I believe it was the third week when

John came right out and asked, "When do we get your peace, when will that happen for all of us?"

Unfortunately, there is no formula or quick how-to-instructions. All I could do was share my story and invest myself in theirs. The amazing transformation that took place from there, you will have to read for yourself in this book.

As I write this, I realize our first meeting was over several years ago. They have since become two of my closest friends, and I can't imagine my life without them. I am thankful to Baby Jake for bringing me his parents. It was his brief presence in this world that allowed our paths to cross. It breaks my heart that they weren't able to keep him here on earth. Although, I've heard it said: when you know where something is, it isn't really lost. We will see our babies again, but until then, God gave us each other.

This is their journey in healing and discovering their purpose...and it will inspire you.

Kim Preston
Angel Mom to Jeremiah
& Founder of In His Arms

Introduction

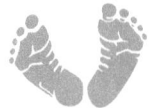

When your eyes have been opened to pregnancy loss, there is a common notion that this is only happening to you. Although statistically, it happens to one in four women. So, why is there so much taboo around this subject? Often couples feel the shame and blame and choose to keep silent. This was us. We felt we were the only ones. We felt lost and alone.

Having suffered a series of pregnancy losses ourselves and now leading a support group for several years, we have come to learn that almost all bereaved parents feel the same way we did. Regardless of the stage of their loss, the devastating pain is the same for everyone. As part of our ongoing support group, grieving parents have written letters to their angel babies. Each letter filled with the hope they anticipated and the heartbreak they felt.

In 2018, our friend, Kim, who was co-leading the group with John and me, identified that these letters needed to be shared. When John and I were grieving, we found comfort in reading other people's stories of personal loss. Their letters validated what we were feeling and going through. We felt less alone in our grief and knew the letters we heard in our support group would provide the same comfort for someone else. The idea of a book was born. After meeting with several editors and publishers, we learned a collection of letters alone was not enough to make a book. Readers needed to hear our story—a couple who was broken and lost, yet arose from the ashes. A couple who believes God has a greater purpose for all our babies in heaven. We made a promise to the angel moms and dads in our group–their babies' stories will not be forgotten, and they will bring comfort to the broken-hearted. This book is the result of that promise.

In *Dear Baby, Our Angel We Lost, Love and Honor Forever,* we hope to bring comfort and peace to those on this grief journey. In addition to our story, each chapter provides a unique insight into the often unshared dad's perspective. Our goal is to not just comfort the women, but the men who typically sit on the sidelines and grieve silently. Some sections may resonate with you more than others, while other sections may provide insight into what escaped you. At the end of each chapter, reflect on your takeaway; may it guide you in your own journey of living in your new normal.

Introduction

We wish it wasn't necessary for anyone to read this book. Sadly, loss happens. If you, or someone you know, has suffered a miscarriage, stillbirth, or neonatal loss, this book is for you. You are not alone. We hope this book helps you move forward in your journey and may it bring you comfort however long your own grieving process takes.

"There is no shame in grieving.
You grieve deeply because you loved deeply."
–Tani Leeper

CHAPTER ONE

It Shouldn't Be This Hard

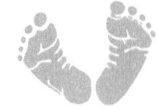

"One day you will tell your story of how you've overcome what you are going through now, and it will become part of someone else's survival guide." –unknown

One can never be prepared to hear the words, "There's no heartbeat." There is nowhere in the pregnancy handbook that the nurse gives you after your initial prenatal visit that prepares you for such an outcome. Yet, it happens to one in four women. Wait, what? Really? How was I never aware of this? I was so naïve in thinking, having had a successful pregnancy in the past, all pregnancies are just like it.

As a schoolteacher, I routinely had a wellness checkup prior to a new school year. It was the end of August 2011, and John and I had just celebrated our eighth wedding anniversary, when I went in for my routine physical exam. I figured just like all the other visits in the past, it would be a quick answer to some questions, check a few boxes, provide a sample here and there, and take deep breaths—inhale...exhale, done. Nope, not this time. There was something extra special about this trip. I asked my doctor to run a pregnancy test because my period was a little weird that month. A few minutes after providing a urine sample, my doctor walked in and said, "Congratulations, you are having a baby."

John's jaw slightly dropped, I looked at him with eyes open wide in disbelief, and it took a minute for the shock to set in before we were overcome with excitement. Our eyes welled up, and I whispered to him, "We're going to have a baby." This was definitely a surprise as we didn't plan on having children of our own. We were happy with just the two of us and raising my daughter, Samantha.

But the bliss from our unplanned pregnancy was short-lived. Eight days later, at eight weeks pregnant, I started spotting, which turned into slight bleeding. To err on the side of caution, we went to the emergency room to make sure everything was okay. After what seemed like several hours waiting to be seen by a doctor, we were finally escorted into an exam room. Laying there, I was feeling anxious about the unknown, but nothing prepared me to hear the words,

"There's no heartbeat." I remember I wanted to cry, but I didn't know if I should. What do you do at a time like this? I felt sad and confused. I was given a choice to schedule a D&C (dilation and curettage) or allow the miscarriage to happen naturally. I chose the latter.

A few days after our emergency room visit, the miscarriage process started, and we did not even get to hear our baby's heartbeat. We were pregnant for such a short time, yet why was I feeling so sad? The feeling of sadness lingered with me for months, and I noticed John did not share the same feelings I had; I was deeply hurt, and I felt alone. When well-meaning family and friends would say, "It's probably for the best," or "You can try again," or "Try not to think about it," I didn't know if I was angry, sad, or both. Part of me felt their words were dismissing my loss, my pain. Those words hurt. I wish they would have simply said, "I'm sorry" and hugged me, or let me cry with them. At that moment, all I wanted to do was cry. I didn't want to cheer up, or be happy, or look on the bright side. There is no bright side to pregnancy loss.

If a miscarriage was not hard enough to deal with by itself, dealing with people who viewed my loss as a fetus and not a baby, made matters worse. We weren't told we were having a fetus; we were told we were having a baby. I have come to realize that when a pregnancy is going well, the term "baby" is used freely and is acceptable; but once it's not, the term "fetus" is used more than one prefers to hear. I know I was only eight weeks along. I know I didn't get to hear a heartbeat. I know I wasn't even planning to have a baby. Nonetheless, my baby mattered to me, and there is no shame in loving a baby I had never met. This baby made John and I realize how wonderful it would be to have a child of our own. Baby Jul, as we later named our first baby, planted the seed in our hearts to try again.

So, I went through a miscarriage and have come to know what that is. What I did not know about was stillbirth. Are you kidding me, I am going to lose another baby? This time my loss paralyzed me. It was so profound that John grieved alongside me. We did not know how to navigate this brand-new pain.

John and I didn't realize that trying to get pregnant was going to be so challenging. We didn't know that there is such a thing as secondary infertility. It was emotionally taxing to have a body that could not do what it was designed to do. From the beginning, we made a personal decision to only try to conceive naturally. It took one year and ten days for us to get another positive test result. I remember waking up one Sunday morning in early September to take a home pregnancy test. Afraid to disappoint John, I had to be sneaky and wait patiently for the result. When I saw the two pink lines, I was ecstatic. "Finally," I whispered to myself. John was sitting in the family room watching television. I walked over and sat next to him and casually handed him the test result. We were both in tears and disbelief. The rest of it was a blur, I don't even recall how I shared the news with Samantha.

We were cautiously overjoyed. Having already gone through a miscarriage, we could not view this pregnancy with the same innocence and excitement as we did before our loss. Don't get me wrong, the feeling of excitement and joy was still there, but now they were combined with fear, confusion, and sadness, too. We were afraid we were going to miscarry again, so I was careful not to get emotionally invested. I recollect saying to myself, "Don't get too excited about this one." But who was I kidding? I loved this baby from the minute I found out I was pregnant. I have learned there is no such thing as not getting "emotionally attached." I had already saved a space in my heart for this baby even before I saw those two tiny pink lines.

Being cautious, we agreed not to share our news with anyone except John's parents. In my mind I thought, if I can only get through the first eight weeks, we're good. Then, we made it to the end of our first trimester; we were golden. On the 10th of December, we announced on social media that our little family was expecting the arrival of a baby boy in May 2013. The day after the announcement, I went in to see an on-staff obstetrician at the hospital regarding some bleeding and light cramping. I was reassured it was nothing to be worried about and my symptoms were normal. I shared how my stomach felt so full and heavy and was again reassured all to be normal.

Life was going as "normal" as it could be. Then one day, a pregnancy that I was reassured to be going well turned into a three-week fight to save my baby's life. It was two days after Christmas, and I was a little over 21 weeks when the outer membrane of my amniotic sac prematurely ruptured. It was late in the evening and I was getting ready to get into bed when I felt like I had wet myself. I was not sure what was happening. I was not in any discomfort or pain. I was concerned but not alarmed enough to do anything, so I went to bed.

The following morning, the feeling of wetting myself continued, so I called the advice nurse and was directed to come in. John and I arrived at Labor and Delivery and were shortly admitted to a room where they ran some tests. Not long after it was confirmed I had suffered a premature rupture, we were advised to terminate our pregnancy. Again, words no one is prepared to hear. We were in shock and unprepared to make a decision. I told John to phone my aunt and my younger sister, who are both nurses, and share what was happening. After speaking with them, we opted to wait until the morning to decide.

Morning came, and we just could not go through terminating the precious life growing inside of me. A life that was already so loved and we had long been waiting for. We could hear his strong heartbeat and feel his kicks. We could not bear the thought of ending his life. My doctors mentioned I would be transferred to another facility where they have a neonatal intensive care unit (NICU) better equipped for

Jake's early arrival, if I could just make it to 24 weeks. That was the hope I was hanging on to…make it to 24 weeks.

Our fight to keep our baby alive began. Despite the regular visits from the perinatologist—a doctor of maternal-fetal medicine—who repeatedly told me, "You have a nonviable pregnancy and you need to terminate your pregnancy," I continued to hang on. Her words were perhaps one of the most unsettling things I had to process while I was laying in my hospital bed. What she was saying was my baby was a tissue, and even if he survived, he would have all sorts of mental and physical disabilities. I was dumbfounded. Truth be told, at the beginning of our pregnancy John and I were willing to terminate at the first sign of genetic defect, but now faced with it, we couldn't end his life. To me, Jake is my baby and not a tissue. To me, my baby is real regardless of viability or disability. What she was saying may be the truth in the medical world, but she failed to realize that she was speaking to a mother. A mother who did not see the baby growing inside of her as a tissue. A mother who already loved her baby as he was. I wish she could have been emotionally sensitive and more compassionate.

Each day and night, I laid on my hospital bed and tried to focus on making it to the 24th week. Praying to God to save my baby, recruiting friends and family to pray on my behalf, reflecting on life, trying to stay positive, and focusing on little milestones. At each nightfall, I felt I had conquered another day; another win for us. On the 11th

day of my hospital stay; I began to have contractions. I thought Jake was coming on his own will, but it stopped. I was elated to have another day to keep him growing safely inside my womb. On day 13, my doctors spoke to John and me. A decision to terminate my pregnancy needed to be made. We could no longer wait until the 24th week. My white blood cell count was rising, indicating my body was fighting off an infection, and I started to have an elevated body temperature. John and I wept. We did not want to lose our son. I wanted to keep fighting and keep him safe. In tears and feeling emotionally defeated, I reluctantly agreed to be induced.

Jake's chances of surviving the birth were very slim. According to my doctor, if I delivered him alive, they would not sustain life. Although I had known about this for over two weeks, it was difficult to process the idea. It was my job to protect my son, and I failed. I started contractions on my own before the procedure to induce even began. To this day, it brings me comfort to think it was Jake's way of letting me know it was time. It was his way of helping me ease my guilt. This time it was my unborn son trying to protect me. I was physically and mentally exhausted. I feared I was not making the right decision. John and my daughter, Samantha, stayed by my side. My sisters and my in-laws were there too, giving comfort along the way.

It was in the early morning of January 11th, marking the 24th week of my pregnancy, when my baby boy, Jake, quietly

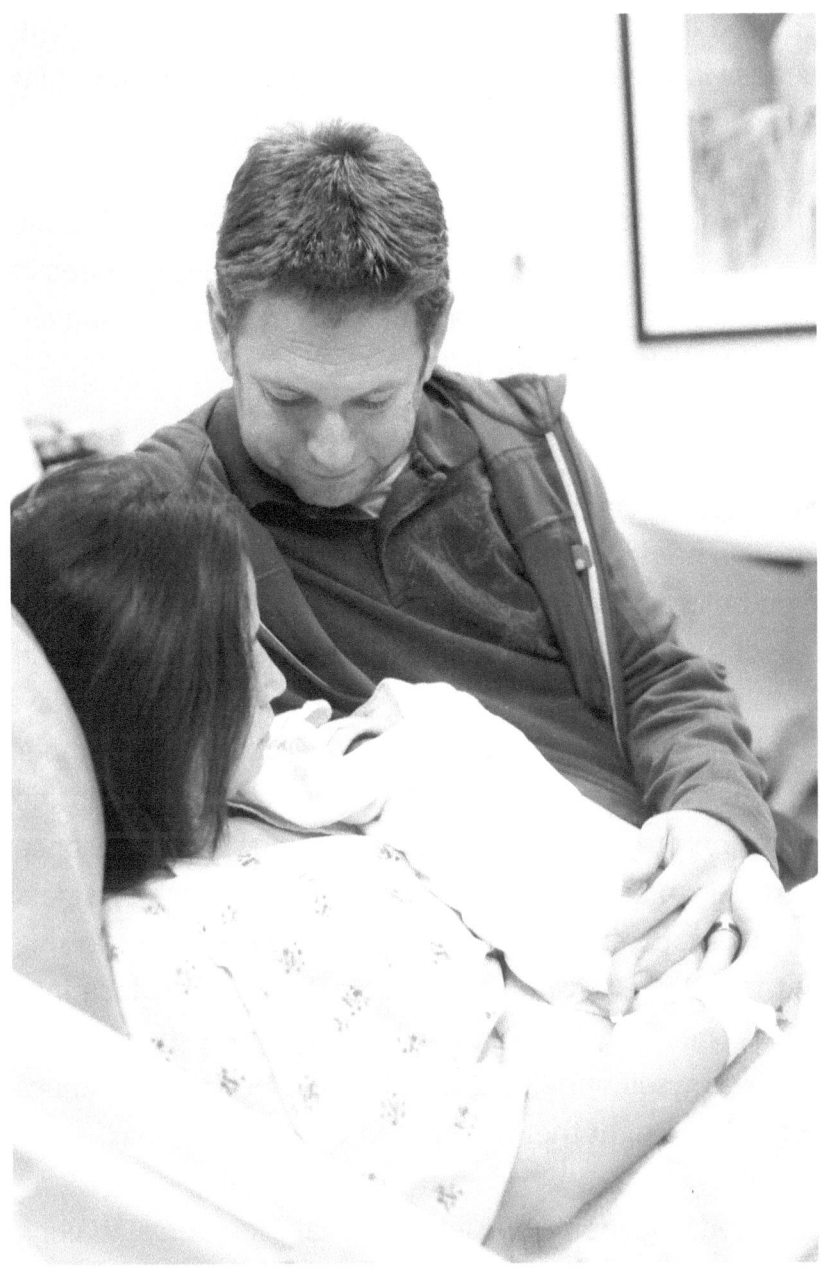

entered into this world. I may not have known this then, but as I look back now, my life as I knew it changed in that moment.

The pain of losing Jake was so unbearable. As much as my heart ached for a baby, I said never, ever again. But deep in my heart and in the quiet moments of my prayers, I longed to hold a baby in my arms.

We did not want to try again, but at the same time, we did not prevent trying again. Over two years later, we got another positive home pregnancy test. I remember I took the test right before a planned business trip to Las Vegas. With the fear of suffering yet another loss, I called my doctor's nurse from my hotel room and insisted to be seen right away. Upon my return, I immediately saw my doctor. I remember walking in hopeful to see my little jellybean growing inside of me, only to be disappointed. Hearing my doctor say once more, "I am so sorry," did not bring me comfort. I just laid on that exam table with tears rolling down my face. Walking out feeling devastated once again, I buried my face into John's chest. My legs felt weak. I didn't have the strength to keep myself upright, and slowly I slid down to my knees and sobbed right there in the hallway.

I decided to go home and let nature take its course. Waiting for the passing to happen naturally left me feeling physically broken and emotionally exhausted, but still clinging to hope that the diagnosis was somehow wrong. Sadly, exactly 30 days from the day I found out I was pregnant, I suffered yet another miscarriage. This time the way I grieved was different and how John responded to my grief was different. Having gone through a support group, I felt better equipped to acknowledge and identify my emotions. It did not take away the sadness, the feeling of defeat, or the shame of having gone through another loss, although I wished it did. Instead, what it allowed was the acceptance and recognition for me to feel the range of emotions that miscarriage brings. This time I leaned on God. I sat still, praying, and waiting for Him to reveal Baby Jo's purpose.

What I have come to know:

- There are some things I simply cannot control no matter how much I plan and prepare.

- There is no such thing as "not getting emotionally attached" to your baby. The love and bond are present from day one and only grow stronger over time.

- Early miscarriages are often dismissed, making you feel you do not have the right to grieve, but you do. You have every right to grieve the life you love and lost.

FROM DAD'S VIEW

How did I end up here? When I was in my late twenties and early thirties, children were the last thing on my mind. Tani and I agreed early on that we did not want to have children together. Truth be told, I was scared of being a father. I was scared of being accountable to raise another life. I felt unequipped for a responsibility of that magnitude.

Summer of 2011 was when I first heard the words that would ultimately change the course of my life forever. "Congratulations, you are pregnant." Obviously, the doctor was not referring directly to me, but I instantly felt warm all over. I didn't know how to react. I was shocked and excited, but looked to Tani to get a feel as to how I should respond. I know that my emotions got the best of me and I started to get teary-eyed. I remember her telling me, "We are going to have a baby." Looking back now, I see how innocent and naïve we were to what lay ahead.

The next week seemed to be a whirlwind of emotions, just living in the moment and soaking up all the goodness that comes with knowing you are going to be a father. Unfortunately for us, that joy was short-lived, and we lost our baby. I was sad and felt defeated, but not like I had lost a child;

more like I had lost a championship game. Running through my head was, "Better luck next time," and "We'll get them next year." Clearly, I didn't bond with the baby like Tani did. I was disappointed, but I wasn't grieving. I couldn't understand why she was so devastated and sad. For me, the loss happened and now it was time to move on. Looking back, I just "didn't get it." I wish now I had been more sensitive and understanding to what my wife was going through.

This pregnancy sparked a desire in my heart to want to try again. I was ready to try immediately, but Tani needed time to grieve. I worried that as time passed, she wouldn't want to ever try again. It took us a little while, but a year later, we were finally pregnant. She surprised me with the news and I was cautiously optimistic. Knowing that the outcome could be the same as before, I was scared. I felt like I had to hold my breath each day, worrying that this might be the day that things go wrong.

As the weeks went by, my worry was replaced with optimism. We made it through the first trimester and found out that we were having a boy. An answer to my prayers. I love my father and the relationship we have, and I wanted to have that with my son. It was neat to watch my wife's belly grow and feel Jake move. I felt that everything was falling into place; we were going to have our perfect little family, our perfect little life. The life I didn't know I even wanted. Unfortunately, late December that year, my vision was shattered.

We found ourselves in the hospital with doctors telling us that we needed to terminate our son's life. I was completely out of my element and was scared to make the wrong decision. I have always trusted and followed doctors' orders, but this time I was not about to give in that easy. Tani and the baby were both stable, so we did not need to rush into any decisions. We decided that we were going to dig our heels in and fight for our son, who was still very strong and active inside of her.

For the next 18 days, I would be on the sidelines. We were fighting for our son, but Tani was in the battle. I felt helpless; all I could do was stand by and watch as she endured the physical pain of needle pricks, sleepless nights, and the emotional pain of potentially losing a baby. I was her cheerleader, trying to keep her spirits up, spending every minute with her. Truth be told, many times the encouraging words that I would tell her I didn't even believe myself. I would go on walks outside and cry so that she wouldn't see me break down. Amazingly, she, who normally has a pain tolerance of zero, was so strong and brave the entire time. I gained a new respect and love for her over that period.

Early in the morning of January 11, 2013, our son Jake was born still. It was the most beautiful, yet saddest experience of my life. The three weeks leading up to it had prepared my heart and mind for what could happen. I took everything in and didn't want to miss a thing. After all the commotion had stopped, everyone had left the room, and Tani was sleeping, I spent a few hours holding Jake and just talking to him. I let him know how much I love him, how I will miss him, how I wish things were different, how strong he was to hang in there with his mom and hoping he didn't suffer. Looking back now that time was priceless; the moment provided me with the closure I needed to say to good-bye to him.

Leaving the hospital with empty arms was hard. Like a brand-new dad, I was supposed to be fiddling with his car seat for the first time while he was snuggled safely in it. Why did this happen to us? How would we pick up the pieces and try to put our life back together? We had so many questions and very few answers. We spent the better part of two and a half years trying to move forward in a healthy manner and decided to give having a baby one last try. Maybe this time it would work out for us.

One night I came home from work to find a positive pregnancy test on the dresser, and I immediately said, "Oh no." No kidding, those were my exact words. It was a response perhaps someone who unexpectedly got his girlfriend pregnant would say. I was excited for us, but also so scared that we would have to admit defeat again. We were cautious, but at the same time wanted to embrace this life. Despite trying to stay positive, praying, and providing the best prenatal care possible, we lost our third baby. Unlike the first miscarriage, I was in a different place and knew exactly what Tani was feeling. We worked through our grief and feelings together and worked on coming to an acceptance that having children on this earth is probably not in our cards.

Tips for Dads:

- No matter in what gestational stage the loss of your baby, take the time to grieve and support your partner for as long as needed.

- When your gut is telling you that something is not right with your partner's pregnancy, seek medical advice right away.

- If you suffer a stillbirth, I encourage you to hold your baby. Once that opportunity passes, you will never get it back again.

CHAPTER TWO

The Unimaginable Reality

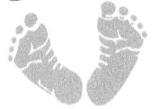

"Mothers have an innate drive to protect their children from any harm, and inevitably feel guilty if they can't achieve that." –Julia Bueno, M.A.

We were getting ready for the arrival of our baby boy. We picked out his crib, furniture to fill his nursery, pre-registry, tiny baby socks and blankets, but we were not prepared for the arrival of his death. Prior to my induction, John's cousin Sara had arranged for a photographer to come after I delivered. I did not know what to think of it. After being told for so many weeks Jake was a tissue, I didn't think my baby was worth being photographed. As Sara was arranging this behind the scenes, John's brother and his wife gave us a baby ink print set during their visit. I would not know the significance of these things until later.

I tried my hardest to keep Jake safely in my womb for as long as I could, but the moment I dreaded had arrived. For some reason, I had this feeling that when I delivered Jake, it would be in the middle of the night. I don't know why, perhaps a mother's intuition? Just as I suspected, Jake came into this world at 1:28 in the morning. He was very quiet and still. I was scared to look at my own baby; I was afraid I wasn't going to recognize him. He was referred to as a tissue for so long, I didn't know what that looked like. But when the nurse finally laid him on my chest, all my fears faded away. He looked like a baby, not like a tissue as I imagined.

I cried. He looked so bruised and tired. His tiny little body had fought hard to stay strong inside of me. He was so brave. As much as I wanted to hold him longer, I couldn't. The morphine had not completely worn off, and I soon began to doze off. John said Jake's grandparents, aunts, and sister stayed to spend time with him through the early hours of the morning. What a special moment that must have been.

When I woke up the following morning, Jake was in his bassinette, and John was still asleep; he was so exhausted from the day and night before. The first thing I asked the nurse was to hold my baby. Looking back now, I had no idea how fortunate I was to still have Jake in the room with us. The time I dozed off after delivery could have been the last I saw of Jake. God must have been watching over us.

As I waited for what to expect next, I snuggled with my son. Having no idea how much time I had left with him, I wanted to savor the moment. I studied his little face and body so it would be etched in my mind. He had a button nose like mine. Big ears like his daddy's. His eyes were puffy and shut tight. His skin was wrinkly and his mouth slightly open, like an angelic choirboy. He had blondish eyebrows and big hands and feet. He was our little boy. Staff and family began to trickle in, and the tranquility of my bonding time with Jake was disrupted.

The photographer Sara arranged from the organization Now I Lay Me Down To Sleep arrived. Although I told John to advise her not to come, I'm glad he decided otherwise. John knew how much I would appreciate it later. As I look back, I am so glad and thankful the photographer was there to capture Jake as perfect as he was, and every single person, every single space, every single moment, and every single memory. The photos taken from that morning are my treasured keepsakes of the short time I had my son here on earth.

As it got later in the afternoon, it was time to leave labor and delivery and move back to the room I had been staying in for the past two weeks, RM 3105 in the postpartum unit. I got to keep Jake with me in the room for a while. Again, at the time, I did not know how long I would get to keep him, so I just held him. Slowly the room became empty; only Jake's dad, sister, and grandparents were left. I had time with my thoughts again. You know when a baby is first born, the nurse would take the baby's handprints and footprints? To my surprise, they do this for stillborn babies too. Sadly, the nurse caring for Jake that morning did not capture the best prints, and I did not know if I could ask her to redo it. So, I accepted what was. Thankfully, John's brother and his wife had the foresight to leave behind an ink print kit, which gave me an opportunity to retake Jake's prints. With Samantha's help, we carefully pressed his right hand on the black inkpad and onto the white paper, then repeated this for his left foot. They turned out perfect. His little right hand and his little left foot perfectly captured in ink. That was a special moment in time with both of my children.

By now, it was about 2:30 in the afternoon, and I had to hand over my baby to Nurse Nancy. We said our goodbyes as we all sobbed. As sad as this moment was for all of us, I also witnessed one of the most touching moments of my life. Jake's grandpa is a man of very few words and does not often display his emotions, but that afternoon, he wept. He wept for his grandson, and he wept for his son.

The Unimaginable Reality

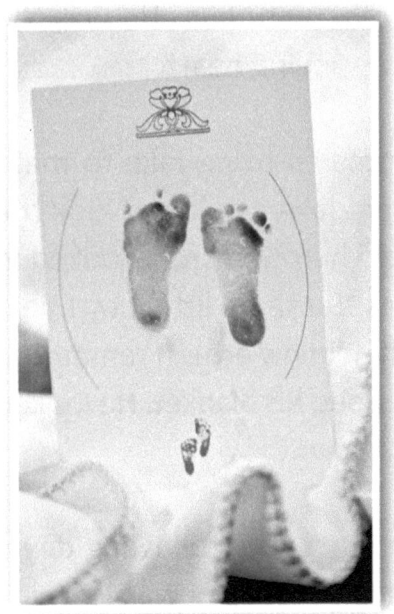 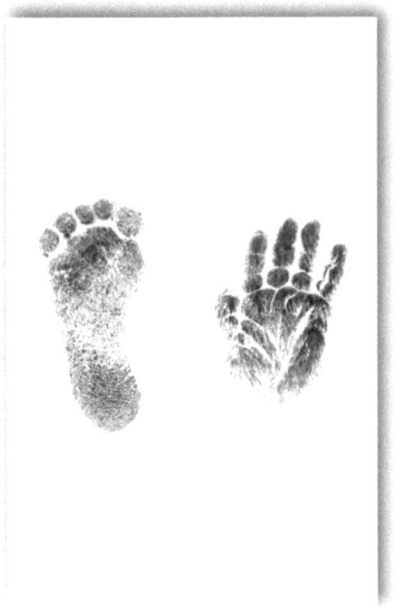

The night brought deep sadness. As everyone left and John had fallen asleep, I felt so alone. I missed Jake. Would I ever get to hold him again? I wanted him back with me, if not growing safely inside of me, safely in my arms. I cried. I cried hysterically in pain. Pain that I had not felt before (I learned later that what I felt was grief). I cried myself to sleep that night, which was the first of so many similar nights to follow.

Morning came, and John had to leave for work. Samantha came to stay with me. I couldn't stop thinking of Jake. I tried to stay strong but eventually began to cry uncontrollably again. I wanted to hold my son, but what would he look like at this point? I didn't know how a dead baby looked the day after delivery. I was apprehensive to ask for my baby, but I knew I needed to be with him. He was the only one who could soothe my aching heart.

Samantha asked Nurse Gemma to bring Jake to me. I am not going to lie, I was afraid Jake would not look the same as he did when I first held him. Samantha looked at Jake first to make sure he was the same little boy I held yesterday, and then she laid him in my arms. I remember he was so cold. I slowly unwrapped his blanket. He looked so precious, better than I imagined.

Holding Jake brought me comfort. The following day, I was braver to ask for him again. Perhaps I was learning to be a mother to my dead son. Every moment I had with him was a gift. Today, those moments are a part of my treasured memories.

Day two of postpartum, it was now the 13th of January, and the following day was Samantha's 22nd birthday. I didn't want her to spend her birthday in the hospital, and I knew it wouldn't be much of a celebration for her if I were still in there. The only reason why I would stay longer was to have more time with Jake. There was never an "enough" for me when it came to holding my son. Against my doctor's wishes, I left the hospital that evening. I wanted to take Jake with me. It was tormenting to know I could not take him home. It felt like there was a heavy weight on my chest; I couldn't breathe, yet tears were uncontrollably running down my cheeks. It was so unfair that other moms got to take their babies home and I couldn't.

The drive home was nothing but tears. Arriving at the house, I felt anxiety. Walking into our home for the first time in 18 days, and no longer pregnant, felt sad and empty. I remember my father-in-law saying, "The sooner we can get back to normal, the better." I didn't know what normal looked like anymore. There was nothing normal about what I was feeling. I wanted to believe him, I just didn't know how. Jake was supposed to be right there with me, with all of us. I held John's hand tightly and clutched the Baby Jake bear my sister gave me for Christmas, as I laid in bed sobbing until I fell asleep. Perhaps this was my new norm?

Another day was before me. It was Samantha's 22nd birthday. I wanted to do what Dad said, get back to normal. So, what would I usually do on my daughter's birthday? We celebrate, that's what we do. I wanted to be strong for her. I went to the nail salon with my mother-in-law and Samantha to get some pampering. I tried to feel normal, but I didn't. I found myself getting teary-eyed every so often and holding back the tears. The ladies at the salon learned about Samantha's special day. One of the ladies asked if Samantha was my only child. This was the first time I was asked how many children I have; I froze for a second, I wasn't prepared to share, but I didn't want to deny his existence. I replied, "No, I lost my son last Friday."

It was silent after that, but I was glad no one brought up any more questions. It took all I had in me not to fall apart.

That evening we went out to dinner with family. I tried my best to act normal for everyone at the table, but it was so hard. Not only was I dying emotionally, but I was also enduring the physical pain that came with post-delivery. I was sitting there with ice packs wrapped around my chest. My body was producing milk for a baby that I was supposed to have. The pain was excruciating.

Day four after losing my son, plans needed to be made for his final services. The fact that I knew Jake had a very slim chance of making it did not lessen the grief, nor did it make me more prepared for his death. In the midst of my grief, I was trying to figure out what a parent is supposed to do when their child dies. First, I had to figure out what I wanted; understanding what I wanted helped me decide how I was going to move forward. I knew I wanted Jake home. I knew I wanted a funeral home that had all their services in-house. I knew I wanted a lasting, tangible piece that represented my son's brief presence here on earth. Behind our burden of sorrows, John and I were forced to do our research. We had to make quick decisions and hoped we made the right ones.

John and I made arrangements for a mortuary to pick up Jake from the hospital. I remember feeling "this makes it all real" and feeling anger, sadness, and hate all at the same time. I hated that I had to plan Jake's cremation service instead of planning his coming home. I hated that I had to decide on an urn and return his crib. I hated that instead of a nursery, my son had a refrigerated locker: locker number 1E0306. I hated that I would miss out on so much with my son.

The day after Jake was picked up and moved to his final resting place, I requested to see him. When John and I walked into the viewing room, there was our little boy's tiny fragile body in what seemed like a huge room. He was lying on a table nicely arranged with baby blankets. Seeing the love and care they took to present our boy to us was heartwarming. It didn't take long to realize that John and I made the right decision in choosing Jake's final resting place.

Sonya, the mortuary technician, was God sent. She guided me on how to be a parent to my dead baby. She told me I could find an outfit for Jake and dress him. She said John and I could decorate his cremation box. She told me I could visit Jake as often as I liked. Every time I visited, I took pictures—lots of them. During my first visit, I arranged for a lady to take molds of Jake's hands and feet. The pieces Monica created have become one of my most-loved treasures today. I am forever grateful for these two ladies.

Jake's cremation came and went. Another chapter in my boy's journey had come to an end. The days after, I felt, were one of the darkest times. Now what? While I was awaiting Jake's cremation, I had a purpose, each day I got up to visit him. Now my days did not have purpose. Nothing seemed important. Nothing seemed to make sense. Getting out of bed was hard. Many days I stayed in my pajamas all day. I scoured the Internet. I read other people's stories of loss so I could understand my own and so I didn't feel so alone, or crazy for that matter. As much as I wanted life to stop, it didn't, and trying to function in it was nearly impossible. I found myself going through the motions of the day but not really knowing why.

When I found myself in the company of others, I tried to be strong. I hid my grief from them as to not make anyone feel uncomfortable. I would wipe my tears away and jokingly excuse it as something else. I would say I was okay when inside I was not. I forced myself to put on a strong front to get through each and every day. When I was alone, my walls started crashing down.

In retrospect, I can see how this was confusing for my husband. John thought that when I was pretending to be strong, I really was okay, so he would carry on trying to function and live our lives as normal as possible. He would go to work, watch TV, and had a healthy appetite when I could barely eat. He would lay his head on the pillow and immediately fall asleep when I would still clutch onto my bear and cry myself to sleep. I felt alone in my grief. I felt he had moved on. I felt he didn't love Jake like I did.

I resented him. Then my resentment turned into anger until one night it exploded into a fight. That fight saved us. We didn't realize how we had been avoiding talking about our grief. I didn't realize he was trying to be strong for my sake. The fight allowed us to get real with each other and come back together.

There is an array of emotions that comes with grief; self-blame, guilt, shame, and anger were just a few that I carried with me. I felt responsible and guilty for what happened. I can recall the guilt I felt with my first miscarriage. The pregnancy being a surprise, I wasn't exactly thrilled at first. Did I subconsciously will my miscarriage to happen? With Jake, I replayed many scenarios in my head of what I could or should have done differently. Was it the bite of sushi that I had? Was it because I was on my feet a lot? Was the occasional small serving of Frappuccino too much caffeine? Did sitting for a prolonged time cause poor circulation and put strain on my womb? Should I have rushed to the hospital as soon as I didn't understand what was happening? Could I have saved my baby? After all, I am his mother; I was responsible for guiding my pregnancy into a healthy outcome. It took time for me to understand that I did not cause the unfortunate end results of my three pregnancies. I have learned that pregnancy loss is not uncommon and often the reasons are unbeknownst to us.

What I have come to know:

- In a state of anger or frustration, we may act harshly or make decisions that we will regret later. I learned not to rush into getting rid of things. I learned to live in my grief for a while before making any quick decisions. I'm so thankful my husband did not get rid of my Baby Jake bear when I asked him. I am glad he didn't cancel the photographer as I asked him to. They are now a part of my son's story.

- Men and women grieve differently. It's not always easy to recognize a man's emotions and definitely not easy to talk about grief. Don't mistake their silence for lack of care, love, or pain.

- After a loss, it is not uncommon for tension to be present in your relationship with your partner. Conflict is normal and can actually lead to a healthy understanding that pulls you closer to each other.

FROM DAD'S VIEW

How do I come to terms with our new normal? Waking up on the morning of January 11, 2013, I had to accept the fact that Jake, and all the plans and dreams that I had for him, had slipped through my fingers earlier that morning. I had to admit my own defeat, but I also knew that I needed to pick myself up and start with the damage control. I needed to protect Tani and make sure that she was going to be okay. I needed to put my emotions and myself on the back burner and focus on her.

The next few days in the hospital, I did what I could to support Tani. The only time that she felt comfort was when they would bring Jake to the room for her to spend time with him. It was always so cute; they would put him in a little basket to transport him, and I can still see her smile each time that basket arrived. Conversely, I can still remember how hard it was for her to say goodbye each time he had to leave. It was such a blessing for me to see the way she cared for Jake, always making sure that he was well cared for and presented in the best way possible.

I began heading back to work and then would go to the hospital in the evening to stay with Tani. The problem was, I was so tired that once I laid my head down, I would fall asleep. Looking back, I know that I failed Tani; she would tell me that the nights were the hardest. She would lay and just cry herself to sleep. I tried everything but could not stay awake. I hate myself for allowing her to have to go through that alone.

It seemed like they would never discharge Tani, all we wanted to do was go home. Finally, we got the all-clear and we were set to leave. This was yet another reminder that our pregnancy journey had ended. Walking out was hard, we were leaving our baby behind, and I wanted to take his body with us. I don't think we said a word on the ride home. I soon realized that from this point forward, there would always be this elephant in the room that no one wanted to talk about.

The next few days, we just wanted to spend time together. I would go to work and Tani would ride in the truck with me, then we would spend time with Jake at the funeral home. We usually got about two hours with him and the majority of the time Tani would hold him while I took pictures. I remember asking her why she wanted to hold him all the time. Tani said, "One day we won't be able to hold him any longer. I want to remember every part of his tiny body." Tani was right, but unfortunately, I didn't realize it until he was gone—probably one of my biggest regrets to this day.

The morning of Jake's cremation was cold and rainy. We had our family gathered with us as we laid him into the box that he would be cremated in. It was so hard to let his little body go; we knew that this was going to be the last time we would ever hold him.

Tani was sobbing with her head buried in my chest. There was nothing that I could do or say that could bring her comfort. It was one of the saddest days I have had to live through.

After the cremation service, we had to wait four hours to get Jake's ashes. I remember having our family around us while we waited, but I felt completely alone. Physically I was there, but emotionally I was in another place. I wished I was still with Jake; I wished our time with him was not over. Visiting him at the funeral home had filled the void in our days, now what would we do? I knew that day would mark the end of another chapter—our time with Jake on earth, and another chapter was just beginning—dealing with the pain.

We received the call that Jake's ashes were ready. We raced over to pick him up and finally bring him home. I was not prepared for the emotions when the lady handed us a single red rose and Jake in an urn, and said, "I'm sorry for your loss." It was over. Our son was now in an urn and this is all we will have to remember him by. I remember walking to the car and all I could think was how much of a failure I was. No one in my family has gone through this. No one I know has gone through this, just me. This was not how it was supposed to end. Why me? How was I going to move forward in life?

Coming home was difficult. My parents were there for a few days and it was nice to have people in the house, although I'm sure we were terrible hosts. The day came when they decided to head home. I didn't know it then, but I was standing on the verge of the darkest days of my life. I felt complete and utter debilitating pain and grief. I could no longer stay busy with the "business" of Jake. I was alone with my thoughts and could not see a way out. I spent day after day sitting on the couch, replaying everything that happened, wondering what went wrong.

This went on for about a week, and then it was time to put it behind me. That is what men do right? We protect the emotions of our partner, and we don't show our own emotions. I tried to show on the exterior that I was moving on but still was a mess inside. I would tell Tani that everything was going to be okay and that everything happens for a reason. I didn't even believe what I was telling her. I would break down and cry in the shower and on the drive to and from work. Guys, this is the wrong thing to do. Nothing good comes from this method, trust me!

One night, things came to a head between Tani and me. She felt that I had moved on and was not grieving Jake any longer. Me thinking I needed to be strong for her was actually putting a wedge between us. Tani expressed to me that she wanted to see me grieve; she gave me "permission" to be vulnerable and show my emotions. She said that we were on this journey together, side-by-side, not one in front of the other. This was probably the biggest turning point for us in dealing with the loss of Jake. It set the groundwork for us, as a couple, and has shaped who we are today and why we feel it is so important to grieve together.

Tips for Dads:

- After the loss of a child, be present for your partner at night, which is when things quiet down and are the hardest for them.

- Men may want to suppress their emotions after a tragic loss, thinking or wishing the pain will go away. In reality, you need to express your pain, may it be in words or tears.

- Guys, we want to fix things, but there is no "fixing" this. Have an honest conversation with your partner so you can understand each other's expectations.

CHAPTER THREE

My Ethereal Love

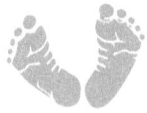

"I don't think most people truly understand how much is lost when a baby dies. You don't just lose a baby, you also lose the 1 and 2 and 10 and 16-year-old he would have become. You lose Christmas mornings, loose teeth, and first days of school. You just lose it all." –Stephanie Paige Cole

The bond a mother has with her baby in the womb begins at the earliest stage of pregnancy. To a majority of women, this bond is almost instantaneous. A mother quickly falls in love with the little poppy seed growing inside, and this bond is strengthened at childbirth. She quickly dreams and imagines the life of her little one, and how her own life will be forever enriched. So, when a loss happens instead of a happy ending, it shocks us to the core.

Although all three losses that John and I suffered were heartbreaking, the loss that crippled us the most was the loss of our stillborn son, Jake. About a week after Jake was stillborn, my sister handed me a bulletin for a miscarriage support group held at a Christian church in Porter Ranch. Feeling alone as if nobody understood what I was going through, and not being able to identify what I was feeling or thinking, I decided to call the number on the bulletin. I spoke directly with the lady who was leading the group. Kim lost her baby boy, Jeremiah, at 13 weeks gestational stage in January of 2012. Seeking purpose through her grief led her to start In His Arms: a six-week support group that helped moms find hope after a miscarriage. Hearing that she too had gone through a loss brought me relief. Here was a real person who had struggled with my pain and not just someone from the Internet or a person from a book. I immediately felt it wasn't just me any longer. I knew this group was where I needed to be, but I was afraid to go alone. Even though the bulletin stated that this was for women, I asked if I could bring my husband along. That decision was a game-changer not only in my grief journey, but in John's as well.

Sixteen days after Jake was stillborn, John and I found ourselves sitting in a support group with our facilitator,

Kim, three other grieving moms, three other grieving dads, and a grieving grandmother. I didn't know what to expect, or what I would gain, all I knew was that I didn't want to feel alone in this grief any longer. Attending this support group was one of the best things we could have done for ourselves and our grief. One of the many benefits of being in a support group is gaining hope and confidence. Meeting others in the group who were further along in their healing journey and had made great strides in living out their new normal showed me that healing is attainable. It gave us a nurturing platform to share what we didn't know how to express on our own. It gave our grief a place to go, and it allowed us to be heard. Sharing our story out loud was empowering, and we found strength and healing in hearing other's stories. The group gave us confidence and renewed hope for the future.

Admittedly, Jake's loss was the driving force behind our attendance at In His Arms. However, one of the many tough questions I was challenged to tackle was: How do I validate the lives lost? This support group taught me that every life in the womb matters—it is valued and has a purpose. So, even though my pain at that moment was greatly focused on the loss of Jake and letting go of the life I once imagined, it also awakened the unhealed wounds from my first miscarriage. A shorter life, but I still grieved.

I sometimes struggle with the thought that my first baby lost in early miscarriage did not get the recognition it deserved.

To most it was unknown; those that came to know about it dismissed it. I felt that my first baby was not valued for its short but significant life. No one talked about it. No one asked about it. No one really grieved the loss but me. Looking back, I have come to realize that is okay. Miscarriage was a concept they had no real understanding of, and neither did I.

Not many people knew about my first miscarriage; we didn't make it far enough to share the news publicly, and the same went for our second miscarriage. But close friends and family knew about Jake—John and I announced on social media that we were expecting our little boy. Many were happy for us and our families bonded with the idea of Jake and welcoming him to our family. John told me that the day I was induced at the hospital, the waiting room was filled with our family patiently waiting to meet him even though they knew he might be born still. Baby Jake was loved before they even knew him.

By my second miscarriage, I had been co-leading In His Arms support group for two years. I had come to understand that life within is life to be celebrated. I had a support system in place with whom I felt safe and comfortable sharing the immediate news. My "grief family" understands the significance of a life lived and lost in the womb, which made the grief of my second miscarriage bearable. My loss was validated without reason, explanation, or judgment, and I was better equipped to openly grieve.

Although each of my losses had been received differently by myself as well as the world, each has led me to understand that my babies' short lives were significant in shaping my new role as a mother to angel babies. Even if people don't recognize it, it is my job as their mother to make their lives matter.

Grieving the loss of my babies was also grieving the shattered plans, hopes, and dreams for their future. Plans for Jake's arrival were set in place; we were over halfway to the finish line. We were getting our finances in order so we both could take time off work to bond with our little one. John and I had chosen a nanny for when I returned to work and we even had the furniture for his nursery set to be delivered.

I had plans of celebrating many milestones such as birthdays and starting school, visits to grandma and grandpa, boat rides with his dad, his big sister teaching him how to play basketball, and celebrating Easter, Halloween, and Christmas. For Jake, I believe the natural grieving of letting go of all of these hopes were compounded by the fact that I also saw this as a second chance.

I was very young when I had my first child, Samantha. I did not have a whole lot and was not in a relationship that I loved. I didn't have a place to call my own, so I did not get to prepare a nursery for her or even provide her with a crib. I was looking forward to doing things differently for Jake. I am in a loving marriage and have the financial means to provide differently. I was excited to create a nursery and had decided on a theme: a light shade of green and cream with tiny turtles, a gray sleigh crib which would later convert into a twin bed, a matching changer dresser, and an upholstered cream striped linen rocker; all symbols of a life forthcoming. These were the tangible things that I was robbed of having and it stings.

Sometimes people could not understand my grief. They could not see past the loss of my babies as the loss of my future with them too. When well-meaning people said to me, "It's okay," "It's for the best," "You can try again," "God needed another angel," or "At least you weren't that far along," it didn't sit well with me, but I learned to give them grace. I would rather they had said nothing at all than downplay the significance of my babies' brief lives to me. They had no clue of what I lost and what I was grieving.

In my own journey, I had to pause and reflect on relationships that were not serving purpose to my healing. It is not uncommon that you too will take distance from some friends and family during your grief journey. It is also not uncommon that you will find new friends who sometimes become your family after loss. Some of my most meaningful friendships blossomed from the tragedy of grief. Don't sweat those who are no longer in your life; focus on the ones who are still standing by you. They are the ones who matter.

What I have come to know:

- A pregnancy loss is not just about losing your baby in the present, it is also losing the future that comes with that child.
- People dismissing my loss has nothing to do with me or my baby. I have learned people are unaware or uncomfortable with facing loss themselves. Give them grace.
- Don't be afraid to ask for what you need in any given moment, the answer may just surprise you and help you in your healing.

FROM DAD'S VIEW

I lost so much more than a baby. After finding out that we were going to have a boy, my mind started running. I wasn't only thinking of the cute little guy that would soon be joining our family, I was thinking of him at five years old riding in the truck with me as I dropped him off at kindergarten. At seven, he would be helping me in the garage, tinkering and disorganizing my tools, or if he is anything like his mom, organizing them instead. At thirteen, he would be out in the boat with me, perhaps trying to impress the girls. And so it went on. I started to see my life with him and imagined what it would be like. I wanted us to have the same relationship that I have with my dad—the kind of relationship where I would be his hero and his best friend all at the same time.

While we were in the hospital, I spent many nights walking the halls to pass the time and I got to know one of the security guards pretty well. One night he said to me, "Congratulations." I was a little taken back and explained to him our situation. I let him know we were having a boy, but things were not looking good. I think to make light of the situation, he asked me if I thought Jake would be a football player when he grew up. My response to him was, "I don't care what he is, he could be a ballerina if he wants, I just want him to come out alive." It was at that moment I realized that all the hopes and dreams that I placed on Jake were never going to come to fruition.

During those dark days that I spent on the couch after we finally brought Jake's urn home, I was grieving those lost hopes and dreams. I spent countless hours wondering how I could turn back the hands of time to get him back. I was faced with the reality that it was over and we may never get another shot at having a child. I started to suppress my emotions in an attempt to help Tani "heal," whatever that looked like.

Tani loved to read stories about others who had suffered the same loss; she found comfort in knowing that we were not alone in this. At the time, we didn't know anyone personally that had gone through a stillbirth; we thought it was fairly uncommon. As we read the stories, we could see the similarity of emotions that all parents feel when they lose a baby. It helped us to identify and sort out the different things we were struggling with. The next thing I knew, Tani had signed us up for a support group at a local church. She told me that it was a group for moms who have suffered miscarriages, but I could also come along. Let's just say that I was not looking forward to it.

I remember walking into the support group and thinking great, I am going to have to talk about my emotions to a room full of strangers, and perhaps mostly women. I was so relieved when I saw a few other dads come in the door with their wives. My fear of being the only guy present was immediately removed. Once we started sharing, I felt a weight being lifted off me. I heard other men confirming and validating my feelings. We had an instant connection and created a bond that will last a lifetime. We would talk for two hours about our loss, and then after group, we would talk in the parking lot about other things in our life. I think we didn't want to leave the company of others who had walked in our shoes. We felt safe in each other's presence.

For the five weeks following that first class, I looked forward to our meetings. I can't stress enough the importance of community when working through your grief. So often I would sit in the group and have this feeling that I could not put the words to, but then it would come to me because of what someone else shared. We would laugh together, cry together, and for a couple of hours each week, we were reminded we weren't crazy.

One thing that I learned from the group was that the bond we share with our baby is real. Admittedly, I did not have a bond with our miscarriages, but I was definitely in love with the idea of them. Those that have never lost a child can't always understand how you can love and care for someone who is not physically here. They also could not understand the grief that I was going through. I heard "It's probably for the best," "You can always try again," and "I'm sure it was going to have problems." I had to give people lots of grace during this time. People say these things to make themselves feel better; if they minimize the event, then they will feel more comfortable around you. I didn't have the strength or the words to explain to them what I was feeling because the emotions were so fresh. Now, however, several years into my journey, I love to get a listening ear. I can go on for hours about the story of my little Jake.

Tips for Dads:

- There is no shame in admitting you love a child you have yet to meet.
- A significant key to healthy coping with loss is finding a good support system to walk alongside you.
- It is okay to openly share your emotions; this is part of your healing process.

CHAPTER FOUR

The First Cut is the Deepest

"When you are grieving, you are fully permitted to take time off from everyday life. You are not responsible for making everyone happy. You do not have to try to fix things. Take time just to be. Time to sit. Time to feel. Time to regain your strength." –Zoe Clark-Coates

I wanted to put life on pause after losing Jake, but the minutes and hours continued to tick away. The best I could do at this time was to get away, and I did. I called it a griefcation; a vacation from my grief. My advice to you: if you can get away from the day to day of surviving your grief, do it! Feeling joy or happiness may trigger feelings of guilt, for somehow it means that you are over your loss or you've moved on. It's quite the contrary—joy and happiness are necessary to keep your sanity. Getting away doesn't make you forget, instead it rejuvenates your soul so you can keep standing. It is not selfish to want to take care of yourself while grieving. Self-care is essential to help lessen your suffering and prevent you from dangerous habits.

I recall that same feeling of wanting to escape when I was in the hospital. The idea that our baby would not survive and the word "tissue" was ingrained in my mind. In my head, I didn't know what that looked like. I was frustrated, angry, and sad. After one of the perinatologist's visits, I told John that after I delivered, I wanted to immediately leave the hospital and go on a road trip. I didn't care where. I just wanted to leave behind what happened and visit new places. Unbeknownst to me, this "tissue," this "bio-waste" that I pictured in my head was a baby with all his parts. I couldn't just leave him. I had to take care of him, even in his death.

Jake's cremation took place in January. His memorial service took place in February. And in March, John and I took a week-long trip to Puerto Vallarta. The stress of grieving took a toll on our relationship. We needed this time to reconnect in a place where nobody knew our story. The sun, sand, water, endless servings of guacamole, and piña coladas were exactly what we needed at this moment. We weren't responsible for making anyone happy but ourselves. Two days after we arrived, we visited downtown Puerto Vallarta. One of the city's iconic landmarks is the Church of Our Lady of Guadalupe. As we entered the ornate iron doors, ahead of us at the altar was a small white casket. I hid my face into John's chest and sobbed. I wanted to hug this little angel's mom. I turned to God and asked, "Why?" I wanted to leave grieving for a while and right there, smack in front of my face, was a bold reminder. What did I need to learn at this moment? Was this just a mere coincidence? I did not really know the answer to my questions. Perhaps it was for me to sympathize with this mom, or recognize her long journey ahead, or for me to reflect on how far I had come since my loss. I guess the saying is true, you can't run away from your grief. Aside from this minor hiccup on our trip, I loved the fact that we did this for each other. It was another step towards bringing us closer.

All the "firsts" presented physical and emotional challenges. I remember the first dinner out John and I had was with our support group friends. With our luck, or call it a test of grace, we were seated across a party of parents with their new babies. Perhaps it was their first dinner out too since they all had their babies and maybe they even met at a "mommy and me" class. As we sat there, we couldn't help but notice their strollers. We recognized the ones we had picked out for our own babies but would never get to use. During grief, seeing pregnant women or hearing of others' pregnancy news was difficult. It brought a sense of jealousy and sadness. Sadness not because they were pregnant, but sad that it wasn't me instead. The first time I passed the baby aisle at the department store, it brought me to tears. The first time I attended a baby shower made me sad, as plans of my own baby shower were taken from me. Attending a baby shower was not my favorite, but I found picking out a gift from the gift registry was worse; even to this day I still struggle looking at a baby gift registry.

If I were to look back at all my firsts and pick my top three, my due date, Christmas, and Jake's heavenly birthday would make the list. During the latter two, my grief was compounded by my fallen relationship with my daughter nine months after Jake's death. I felt I lost both of my children that year.

My due date was May 9th and by then, I had returned to work. With only six weeks left in the school year, I wanted to finish off the year with my first-grade students. Waking up that morning, I felt anxious. If things went as planned, I should have been at the hospital and not getting ready for work. What if I couldn't control my emotions and broke down in front of my students? I prayed. I prayed for strength to get through the day. During my lunch break, I decided to leave campus and go for a drive. John offered to meet me, but I just wanted to be alone. This was unlike me, because any minute I could spend with that man I would take. I didn't know where to go; I couldn't go far since I had to get back to work, although I didn't want to. I didn't want to eat, but knew I needed to. (This is part of grief by the way, being indecisive. My husband would say that this is a part of my personality even before loss, but I think it was worse during grief.) I ended up at a fast food drive-thru. I ordered a small bag of fries and a mocha frappé. I was supposed to be delivering Jake today. I was supposed to be holding this perfect little being in my arms. Instead, I was sitting in my car pondering what should have been. When I returned to work, a bouquet of white roses awaited me on my desk with a note that read:

> *"Tani, Baby Jake is here with us today. He will always be with us, to watch over and protect us. Our baby boy has impacted so many lives in his short time with us. Thank you for such a precious gift. Love, John."*

Receiving the flowers and note were a symbol of my husband acknowledging the challenge of that day. It was comforting for me to know we were in this grief together, hand in hand, and not apart. I believe neither he nor I knew how it was going to unfold. Looking back, my anticipation of how this day was going to turn out was worse than how it actually was. I remained calm and was able to attach a positive memory to what could have been an unpleasant day. Another "first" conquered, and I was still standing.

Christmas by far is my favorite holiday of the year. I love the lights, the decorations, the gatherings, the hustle and bustle at the mall, presents, Christmas movies, and the spirit of Christmas. I remember hosting a party at home. I wanted to feel normal, happy, joyful; something other than sadness. I was done with grief, I thought. But that first Christmas was compounded with other grief unrelated to Jake, and that made the sadness particularly unbearable. I struggled to enjoy my first Christmas. Thoughts of having my seven-month-old Jake and my daughter flooded my mind and for the first time in my life, celebrating Christmas at home was cancelled. I could have insisted on tradition, but sadly this most joyous time of the year was very difficult for me. I wanted to fast forward to the day when I could still remember my son, but no longer be living in grief. We spent Christmas in Discovery Bay that first year. It was simple, it was quiet, there was sadness, there were tears. It was different, and that was okay.

Two days after Christmas, memories of my fight for Jake's life revisited me and marked the countdown to his first heavenly birthday. I had been dreading this day with so much anxiety and anticipation. The events from a year ago danced around in my head replaying the question, "Did I do everything I could to save him?" I kept going back and forth if I should honor this day or just let it quietly pass by.

Initially, I thought I would plan a party for him with guests bringing gifts suitable for a one-year-old to donate to a local charity organization. But with the extra burden of the strain on my relationship with my daughter, I did not have the emotional strength to carry through with it. From planning a big celebration to not wanting to do anything at all, a compromise was reached—a weekend in Pismo Beach. John's parents planned the weekend getaway, and they were there to honor the day with us. Only a handful of people reached out to us on his first heavenly birthday. I quickly realized that well-meaning family and friends who once filled the hospital waiting room and our living room for his memorial service, soon forgot the significance of our little boy in our lives.

Reflecting on the first year of Jake's death, life did not really slow down. While working through my grief and figuring out my new normal, John and I planned his cremation, his memorial, celebrated birthdays, returned to work, celebrated holidays, gathered with friends, attended baby showers, moved, mended relationships, grieved over relationships lost, mourned the death of a friend, made new friends while saying good-bye to some, and planned Jake's first heavenly birthday. As I look back at my photo album from that year, anyone unfamiliar with my story would not be aware of the brokenness I felt inside. The smile I wore on my face was deceiving. I stayed strong for those around me so they did not feel uncomfortable with my grief. I reserved my tears for when I was alone in my stillness or in the safe presence of my support group peers, who I have come to call my grief family.

What I have come to know:

- I've learned that the anticipation of the first milestones are often worse than the day itself. Listen to your heart. Only you know how much you hurt. Only you know how much you can handle.

- It's not selfish to plan a vacation in the midst of your grief. As a matter of fact, it is essential to your well-being.

- It is okay to make new traditions to fit your new normal.

FROM DAD'S VIEW

Ever just want to get away from it all? When Tani and I started our journey in the hospital with Jake, we said that when all of this was over, we were going to get in the car and just hit the road. At the time, a road trip seemed to be a good way to escape and clear our heads. As our journey in the hospital continued, our perspective started to change. We no longer wanted to run away and leave our baby behind; we wanted to stay close to make sure that all his arrangements would be taken care of.

What we didn't understand then was that if we had taken that road trip to get away, our grief would have been waiting for us when we returned. We needed to stay and make the plans for Jake's cremation and memorial service. We needed to have those dark days alone on the couch. We needed to have our emotions come to a head and give each other the permission to cry and grieve together. We needed to live in the fact that Jake was gone and that this was going to be our new normal. We needed time to start the grieving process before getting away.

In March of 2013 Tani booked a "griefcation" for us in Puerto Vallarta. At first, I was a little skeptical about going on vacation so soon after losing Jake. Even the idea of having a good time made me feel guilty, like it was disrespectful to Jake in some way. Now I know that I could not have been farther from the truth. Jake never wanted me to be miserable; I would like to think he finds joy when I am happy. I had no idea the healing that was going to take place on that trip, both individually and as a couple.

There were a few signs and reminders of our little guy while we were vacationing. One in particular was on one of our tours when we witnessed a funeral mass at the iconic church at the city center of Puerto Vallarta. Looking further down the aisle of the church laid a baby casket. Truth be told, I had never seen a baby casket before. This may sound naïve, but until that moment I didn't even think they made baby caskets. I was in disbelief. It was like someone was playing a sick joke on us and would come out and say, "You're on camera."

Our days were filled with lounging by the pool and slowly we began to recognize the usual suspects. Typically, Tani would be first to strike up a conversation and make new friends, but not this trip. This trip we stayed to ourselves and just watched people enjoying their vacation, wondering if any of them were on their griefcation too. Another reminder of Jake was this beautiful baby girl; she must have been around five months old. She always seemed to be at the pool when we were there. She wore her floppy hat and would float around in her pool ring. It made me realize another hope taken from me.

I didn't want our griefcation to end. The view from our room was magical. We had a front row seat to the most amazing sunsets; it was like a week-long dream. I had anxiety about going home. I knew that when we returned, we were still going to be that couple who lost their baby. The beauty in that statement is that we were still a couple; this was not going to break us. We were united and ready to walk our grief journey together. Thank goodness

because we were about to celebrate a year full of "firsts" that I was not prepared for.

There are things that happen to you in that first year that under ordinary circumstances are no big deal, but after losing a baby can leave you devastated. For instance, the first time someone handed me their newborn son to hold. I had to politely remove myself and hold back the tears so as not to make a scene. I was questioning what had just happened and telling myself to get a grip. Was I going crazy? I thought I was good, but now I can't even be around a baby? This was just the start.

The first time you get invited to a baby shower, again, the internal dialogue is real. You want to attend for support, but how can you sit through it while you're thinking about your baby that you just lost? The first time your close friend tells you they are expecting, you smile and say congratulations, but inside are asking, "Why not me?" Deciding whether or not to celebrate the first Mother's Day and Father's Day was a struggle. Am I a father if my son is not living? What about Halloween, Thanksgiving, and Christmas? They are back to back. For me, the hardest three months to get through in the first year were October, November, and December because we were thinking of how things "should be" compared to how they actually were. Jake would have been five months old by Halloween. I imagined what cute costume Tani would have picked out for him. Would I have taken him on his first trick-or-treating or was he too young to go? By Thanksgiving, Jake would have been six months old. We always spend Thanksgiving with my aunt's family. They would have loved him, and he would have been old enough to sit at the dinner table with us. Jake's first Christmas would have been nothing short of him being spoiled. Instead, I watched my wife dress Baby Jake Bear for the different holidays, light his candle in thematic candle holders she had carefully picked out for each month of the year, and rather than holding my son in the annual Christmas family photo, I held his urn.

By far the two firsts that brought up the most anxiety was Jake's due date, May 9, 2013, and his "angelversary," January 11, 2014. What do you do on the day that you were supposed to welcome your child into the world? What emotions were going to surface? How would we react? I didn't know what was expected of me. I wanted to be sensitive to Tani's feelings but did not want to do anything that would trigger her to break down. I remember talking with Tani to try and get a feel for how she was doing. She informed me that she was going to go for a drive for lunch. I wanted to help attach a positive experience to the day, so I arranged a dozen white roses to be delivered to her work. I still remember the phone call she made to me when she received the flowers. I don't remember the exact words of that phone call, but I remember the affection she felt towards me and that was the positive memory I have attached to my son's due date.

As Jake's first anniversary approached, we couldn't really decide on what to do. My parents suggested a spot in Pismo Beach. They shared that they had stopped and spent the night there while traveling home from our house after we lost Jake and it brought them some comfort. We agreed and met them there for the weekend. It was exactly what we all needed. Tani found the perfect necklace in one of the shops, we all got sweatshirts, and had some great seafood. I remember sitting on the roof of the hotel one evening, overlooking the beach, and just letting out a sigh of relief. We did it; we made it through the first year. Driving home, I felt some closure. I didn't have to worry about what the next holiday was going to look like or what emotion the next milestone would bring up. We had conquered our first year!

Tips for Dads:

- Find a change of scenery and take your partner on a griefcation—it can add value to your relationship and bring you closer than you imagined.

- In our relationship, my wife is the planner. If this is the case for your relationship, take a supportive role in brainstorming and planning with her. Whatever you do, don't just sit back and do nothing.

- There are a lot of unknowns in the first year. Don't hesitate to reach out to someone who has traveled down that road who can offer you tips and advice.

CHAPTER FIVE

The Ultimate Test of Faith

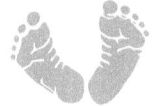

"A tragedy rocks your faith. A tragedy makes you question what you believe. You will not fully understand why bad things happen. But no matter what you do, don't lose hope. Things will get better... this I know. I have survived tragedy." –Tani Leeper

I was born and raised Catholic. Growing up, I attended mass regularly with my family on Sundays and Holy Days of Obligations. I followed the traditional Catholic rituals—confirmation, confession, procession, the rosary, fasting, and the Eucharist. There were statues of saints around my family home, and the fear that God is always watching and will punish the sinners was inculcated in my upbringing.

As I got older, I walked away from the rituals I grew up with as I never fully understood them, but I continued to believe in God. I still prayed and occasionally attended my aunt and uncle's Christian church.

After John and I married, our family of three decided to get baptized at a small Christian church. We attended church every Sunday, then after a while, we fell out of church. I categorized myself as a seasonal Christian with one foot in and the other foot out. I believed and tried to follow the Christian values, but I was lacking the relationship with God that was needed to fully live out my faith.

On the second day of my 18-day stay at the hospital, the hospital chaplain knocked on my door and asked if he could pray over me, John, and our baby. John and I turned him away. He came back the next day, and once again we turned him away. On his third visit we finally agreed to let him in. He delivered the most heartwarming prayer that brought John and me to tears. It was exactly what we needed to hear. He came back regularly to visit and pray over us. Each time he came, the closer I felt to God's words. The morning Jake was born, Chaplain Fred came to meet him. I look back today and realize how little faith I had. I refused this man of God so many times because I didn't know him and felt strange having him get close to my fears and my pain. I recall praying to God, for peace, discernment, and hope, and He brought this man as an answer to my prayers, but I couldn't see it. Chaplain Fred did not match the answer I pictured in my head. What I pictured was my doctor telling me everything would be okay, and Jake would safely be in my arms.

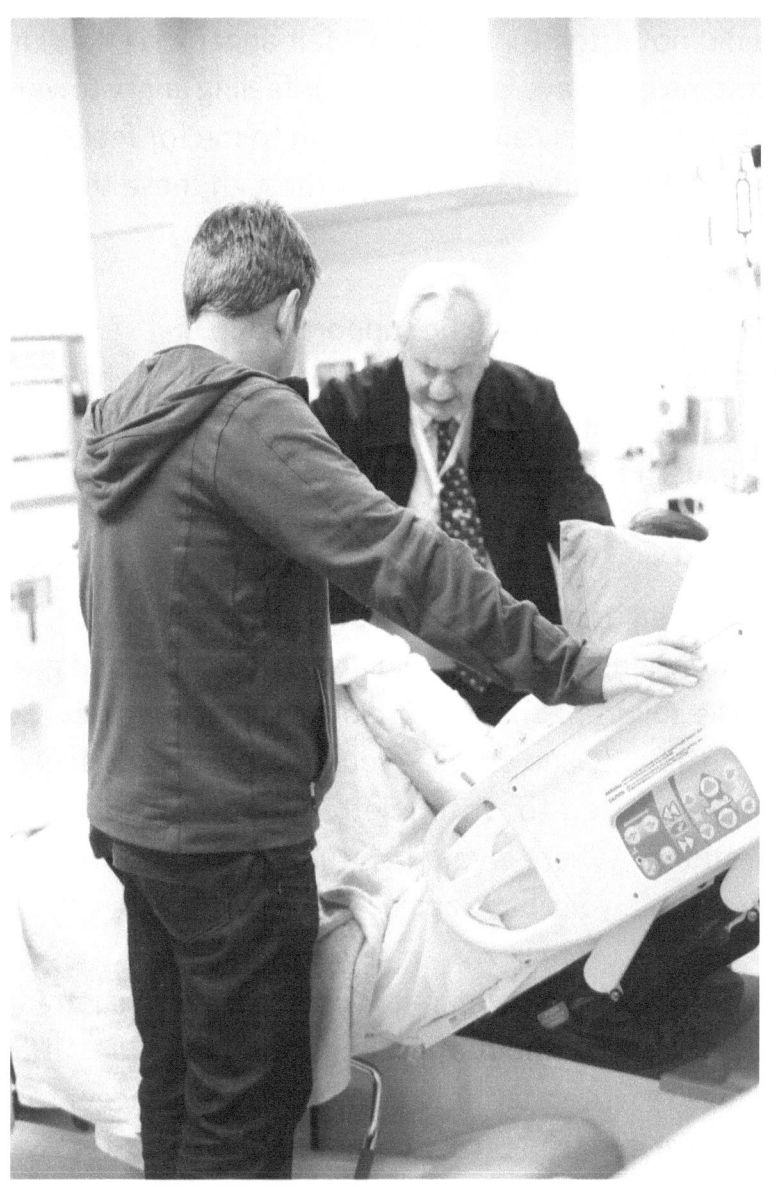

I had so many questions for God. Why did he take Jake so soon? Was He punishing me for my past sins? Was there another way He could have taught me the lesson He wanted me to learn? I felt God had abandoned me; He did not listen to my pleas. I felt anger that He didn't grant me my prayers. I felt fear for feeling angry towards Him; fear He will cause more harm to me for feeling the way I did. I needed help to sort through these thoughts and questions.

It was with the help of the support group that I found the confidence to approach God. We don't realize how God is working behind the scenes. He orchestrates how to equip us in this time of change and growth. He perfectly places people to be present for us as we go through the bad and the ugly as we find our way back to the good. Kim helped us navigate through these questions; she has the knowledge of God's love and compassion and grace for His children. She said it's okay to get real with God for He already knows what you are thinking and feeling. We were asked to write a letter and to reflect on the questions: "Where is your baby now?" and "Do you think you will see your baby again?"

Eager to heal the pain I felt inside, I wrote this letter to God, but not without apprehension or difficulty. It felt strange to write a letter to Him, but it was stranger to let Him have it. Based on my Catholic upbringing, I was not comfortable letting God know that I was angry with Him for allowing me to carry Jake for six months to just take him away. But I knew I had to give it a try. With tears in my eyes and doubts in my heart, I wrote.

Dear God,

I'm trying to understand why this happened to our family. A child we wanted and loved you took away too soon. I feel angry, but mostly I feel sad and full of questions that I may never know the answers to. Why would you allow such a thing to happen? Why would you answer our prayer to simply take it away? Why would you cause us so much pain?

John said this happened to us because you knew we have each other to help us through this very difficult time. You also said that you would not let us go through anything that we couldn't handle, and I believe in that.

You are a good God. I can see your blessings all around me from the start. You have given me a wonderful daughter and an amazing husband who have stood by me. They are my core and my strength. You have given me a family who prayed for me because they love me, a doctor who listened and nurses that nurtured and cared for us. After Jake was born, you made a way for me to spend more time with him than I could have imagined. You continue to work in me to keep me strong.

God, I want to believe there's a reason for my loss and you have a bigger purpose than what I can see before me. I pray that you will guide me on that path of discovery and use my experience according to your will.

Trusting in You,
Tani

After writing the letter, I realized I wasn't as angry as I thought I was. Well-meaning family and friends have said to me, "Focus on the good things that you have or the good things that are happening in your life." I knew what they were saying was true. We know that there is always something to be grateful for, even in the midst of our darkest hour. But in the early stages of our grief, it's hard to see that. Writing allowed me to acknowledge the good things in my life that I may have overlooked when I was so focused on the one bad thing.

The next thing I had to tackle about my faith was the certainty of eternity. I know without a doubt that Jake is in heaven; after all, all babies go to heaven. Addressing the question of whether or not I will see him and hold him again was a little more challenging. When I lost Jake, my relationship with God was nowhere close to what it is today. Although I thought of myself as a "good" person, I wasn't confident that when I died, I would be heaven bound. I did not understand what salvation was. If I wanted to hold my son again, I needed to learn how to find my way to him.

It was doing this assignment that allowed the conversation between God and me to take place, which eventually led me back to the church. I figured I would give this "church thing" another try. I recall attending church service and being in tears the entire time. I felt every song and every message was about my pain. I later learned that is how the Holy Spirit moves; it's a feeling you get in the depths of your soul. Addressing the certainty of eternity challenged me to grow my faith. From attending church, it extended to attending a small bible study group. That small bible study group led to John and me leading groups of our own. From attending the support group, it inspired me to co-lead. I wanted to give back to others what God had perfectly placed in my life during my greatest time of need. I began reading daily devotionals and bible scriptures and listening to worship music, which all brought me hope in the promise that one day I will see my son again. In John 3:16 it reads, "For God so loved the world that He gave His one and only Son, that whoever believes in Him shall not perish but have eternal life." I feel my son's death saved me all over again.

What I have come to know:

- Grief changes you. You will no longer be the same. Some say you are better because of it. Some say you become bitter because of it. I chose to be better. It is through love and goodness that my babies' memories live on.

- Anger is a strong emotion that is usually expressed towards something or someone you are passionate about. Feeling anger towards God means you believe.

- Building a relationship with God is like building any new relationship. The more time we invest, the deeper the trust and intimacy grows.

FROM DAD'S VIEW

Where was God in my darkest days? Being raised in the Catholic church and attending a Christian school growing up, I thought I had a good idea of who God was. As an adult, when it was convenient, I would attend church with my mom. After getting married, Tani and I would attend sporadically, but seemed to lose interest quickly. I carried that same part-time mentality about God with me into the hospital.

When our time in the hospital began, things were coming at us so fast. We were having to make life-altering decisions almost in the spur of the moment. Tani and I called people that we thought could give us guidance to make these hard decisions. Never once did I think to call on God. The chaplain from the hospital knocked on our door every day but we turned him away. I am not sure why he continued to come back each day, but when we hit rock bottom, we let him in.

He came in and just wanted to pray with us and for us. He was a soft-spoken man who had a way of just releasing the built-up tension in the room. I heard his prayers and was respectful of his time, but didn't believe that God was going to listen. He had never listened to me before, He never answered my calls, and He never spoke to me like so many others claimed. I can remember one night asking God, "Why me?" and getting no answer. This was the one time that I needed a miracle and He was nowhere to be found.

After Jake's passing, I was angry with God. I had so many unanswered questions. Questions that only He could answer, but the funny thing was, He and I were not talking. While attending the support group, one of the assignments was to write a Dear God letter. The beauty of this exercise was that it forced me to open up that dialogue. As I wrote, my heart was softened, and my tone changed towards the end of the letter.

Dear God,

This really sucks! We were so excited to have baby Jake join our family. I can't believe you did not allow that to happen. Tani and I have always said, "Everything happens for a reason," and that usually gives us comfort in life's trials and tribulations. Now faced with this tragedy, we continue to say this, but this time I don't understand how it can be true. He was healthy, he was strong, and he would have had a loving home, yet you chose to take him home with you. This is the hardest thing we have ever had to deal with. I am thankful that you are in my life and there for me regardless of the condition of my heart. I ask for your patience and understanding as I go on my journey to peace. I will keep my heart and my mind open to the opportunities that you bring my way along this journey.

Love,
John

Being raised to fear and respect God, it was strange to talk to Him this way. What I learned was that God knows the condition of my heart. He wants me to have a real conversation with Him and talk about my fears, my struggles, and my doubts. This is how a relationship is built, which is ultimately what He wants with all of us. Because the support group was at a church, we started to attend service on Sundays. We would stand at the beginning of service and sing, and I would have tears rolling down my face. The songs spoke directly to my heart: the pain I was feeling, the emptiness, the loneliness, and how God was always there. I felt so close to my son each and every time I stepped into church; a feeling that I just can't explain.

I did not know it, but God had started working on my heart back when the chaplain would knock, yet we would not let him in. I thought He abandoned me, but He was sending His earthly angels my way. He went before me and arranged the support group so we would have a safe place to work through our grief. He gave us a "grief family" so that we could relate and feel normal. He brought us to a dynamic and engaging church, knowing that was what we needed to grow in faith with Him. Then on the way to work one morning, I heard Him softly say to me, "John, it is all going to be okay. You are right where you need to be."

A lot has changed for me since I first walked through those church doors in 2013. I know that Jake was never meant to take a breath in this world, and I am at peace with that. I know that God gave him to us with a purpose, and I live out that purpose every day. I have a love for God and a relationship with Jesus that brings me comfort. Tani and I now lead the support group. He chose us to help others, bring glory to Him, and share with others this peace that we speak of. I have come to realize that God is always listening to my prayers and has blessed me with so much.

I have been asked the question, "What would you rather have, the peace you have now or your son back?" My answer is always my peace. I know God needed to get my attention, and for so long I asked, "God couldn't you have done it another way?" Years into this journey, I know this was the only way. I look back at the old me and I am glad that person has been transformed. God continues to work on me daily, and I am open to His plans for my life. I trust His plans are always better than mine.

Tips for Dads:

- When you find yourself angry at God, don't stop the dialogue. Let Him know your anger—that's how you can start to repair your relationship.

- In grief, do not run away from God, run to Him. This is the time you need Him the most.

- Take time to sit quietly with God so you can hear His answers to your prayers.

CHAPTER SIX

Love, Honor, and Cherish... Always

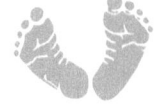

"Sometimes you have to let go of the picture of what you thought life would be like and learn to find joy in the story you are actually living."
–Rachel Marie Martin

"Everything happens for a reason" or "Good things will come from this" are words often shared when bad things happen. I am guilty of expressing these same sentiments to others before. Although I know this to be true, accepting this was not easy. During the dark days of my pregnancy losses, I couldn't see past my tears or feel hopeful beyond my pain. What good could possibly come from such heartache? In the midst of working through grief, I was trying to figure out how everything fits into this new life I am living because "what was" did not fit anymore. I was changing; I was no longer the same. Grief does that.

Over time, while taking positive steps toward my healing, my grief lessened or perhaps I became stronger. The pain is still present, but the gut-wrenching brokenness has dissipated. Having traveled a bit down the road, I can now see how this difficult road led me to a beautiful destination. I was able to find joy, peace, and happiness again, perhaps even better than before my losses. I have come to know of a love that is beyond time and space. I have come to receive comfort that only our Heavenly Father could bring. I learned to let go of meaningless habits and, along with it, people and things that interfered with my ability to live out God's plans for my life. Parents of children with special needs are my newfound heroes. I have come to learn of their courage, strength, and true unconditional love. I have come to embrace the love and support from those I least expected. My marriage has strengthened. John and I developed a deeper and closer connection. Our hearts melded together to endure this tragedy. We came out a stronger and better couple filled with so much hope for our future and love for each other.

I learned my purpose did not end in 2013 after Jake's final arrangements. I found my purpose is to keep Jake's memory alive. His memory is all I have and forgetting him is not an option. Having a child in heaven, I learned, requires a different kind of parenting. I parent by showing love to those in grief, by helping those impacted by loss, by honoring him in our family, by speaking his name and acknowledging his brief existence.

After Jake's memorial, it seemed some family and friends soon forgot about him or perhaps intentionally avoided mentioning him because they feared it would make me sad. Truly, what saddens me is the avoidance. When I hear someone mention my baby's name, I am touched. I may get choked up, not because they made me grief-stricken for bringing him up, but because I am glad they have not forgotten. When family and friends continue to remember alongside me, I am deeply moved. Jake's grandparents send us a card on the 11th of each month. When they return from a trip, they bring back a small souvenir for Jake. Jake's sister, Samantha, signs his name on the Mother's Day, or birthday, or Christmas cards. Friends handcraft personal memorial keepsakes, which adorn the rooms in our home, or gift us a special ornament to add to his growing collection to trim his Christmas tree.

There is a stigma that pregnancy loss should be hidden or kept a secret, as it has been for many, many generations, but I want to break that. In our home, all three babies are present, but Jake is predominantly in every room. People who come and visit our home (whether they have prior knowledge of our losses or not) are aware that we are angel parents. The keepsakes and photos around the house have become "conversation pieces." They help people feel comfortable talking about our babies. Acknowledging the lives lost I held within is part of my healing journey.

There are many ways our family continues to honor, remember, and celebrate Jake:

- Every month on the 11th, we place a single white rose, along with grandma and grandpa's card, by his urn and light his personal "J" candle.

- Each month Jake has a thematic candleholder to decorate his space by my nightstand. For example, a cupcake in January for his birthday, a heart in February for Valentine's day, or a pumpkin for Halloween.

- Every year on January 11th, for his heavenly birthday, we take a day trip and bring Jake's urn along with us. We end the day by sharing a meal with family and friends and blowing out candles on his cake. One of my precious heavenly birthday memories is of my goddaughter, Kailyn, saying in her cute toddler voice, "Happy Birthday Baby Jake."

- We have light blue shirts with an image of his footprint that we wear on his heavenly birthday, or "angelversary." Angelversary signifies the annual date our baby gained his wings.

- We have two special planters in our home that hold seasonal plants. A white tricycle, which John surprised me with shortly after Jake passed, and a green bicycle that I picked up for his seventh birthday. Jake will never get to ride a bike, so these are symbols that bring me comfort.

- In our backyard, there's a particular spot that holds two pots of roses from Jake's memorial service, and with it sits two lighted butterflies. All gifted by family and friends.

- For Halloween, Thanksgiving, Christmas, and his birthday, our Baby Jake bear gets dressed for the occasion.

- Every Christmas, Jake is included in our family photo, and we buy one special ornament to hang on his white illuminated tree.

All these significant things we do in our home and within our circle are comforting and treasured; however, I feel the most significant thing God has purposed our pain for is giving back to our grief community. The very first In His Arms support group ended in March 2013. Due to extraordinary circumstances, Kim planned not to renew the program. John and I knew the need for such a group, and we made a promise to help if she would just continue the group, and so it did.

In 2016, when my teaching career unexpectedly came to an end, Kim handed me the daily operations of the support group. I became a strong force in revising the program, its presence in the community, its image, and rebranding it to what we know it as today: In Loving Arms. I have been told I have a heart for this, and I just may. I wholeheartedly believe in this support group and how it has helped my family and me, and it is my desire to pay forward what I graciously received. God knew what He was doing. It was no accident my teaching career ended, or that Kim was called to embark on a new project, or John and I had to undergo one final pregnancy loss. He chose us because He knew, one day, we would be the comfort to others who would know this same pain.

I never imagined that I would be involved in community work. But here I am pouring my financial resources, time, and talent into managing In Loving Arms. I am truly passionate about growing, transforming, and leading the support group that impacted my life. I love sharing the hope and comfort that I once received to other grieving moms and dads. Leading a couple's group through our church has become a part of our journey as well. Knowing the promise of a God-centered relationship is a hope John and I want to share with others. In addition, Jake's Journey Foundation was formed.

The dreams for this foundation had been in my heart since 2013. It is deeply rooted from my own personal experience. I was not prepared for the financial toll of honoring my son's end of life services, nor the anger I felt towards receiving the hospital bill. I know these things are to be expected, but when you are grieving and just trying to get through each day, the burden that comes with these unexpected expenses magnifies the heartache that you already feel. I felt I was investing so much money for a baby that I didn't get to keep in my arms. I want to spare other parents from going through similar heartache. Jake's Journey Foundation helps families impacted by stillbirth or neonatal death with funeral or cremation services, help continue to fund and expand free support groups for the community, and host the "Wave of Light" event, a yearly gathering to honor all babies lost in the womb and shortly after birth.

Jul, Jake, and Jo's brief existence have made a tremendous positive impact on my life—more than I could have imagined. I now know I am where I need to be.

What I have come to know:

- I used to say to someone in grief, "I wish I could take your pain away." I realized that was selfish of me. I have discovered that my greatest pain revealed my greatest purpose.

- In honoring your baby, try to stay consistent. It takes away the anxiety and guesswork of trying to figure out what to do.

- There is always something to be grateful for, even in the midst of our storm. Find your little blessings every day.

FROM DAD'S VIEW:

Why do bad things happen to good people? Was I being punished for things I have done in my past? These are a couple of the questions that ran through my mind over and over again after the loss of Jake. I have answered each of them a thousand times over while working through my grief. In the early stages, I was convinced that God was punishing me, and if I deserved punishment, then I must be a bad person. Therefore, bad things definitely happen to bad people. I had convinced myself that I deserved the pain I was going through. Now, I can see that I am right where God intended me to be. He was not punishing me, He was molding and transforming me. He was actually rewarding me, and He knew I would answer His call on my life.

I have the advantage of time on my side and have been a part of over 20 support group sessions. I can look back and piece together God's purpose and see the beauty from the ashes. To some of you, this wound may be very fresh, and you cannot imagine how anything good could come from such tragedy. I promise you that if you start to shift your focus, ever so slightly, to look for the little blessings each day, your heart can't help but soften. Once we soften our hearts and let our guard down, we can start to make sense of our loss and find its purpose.

Immediately, I realized my purpose was to keep my son's memory alive. I didn't have a plan on how to do this, but I knew I did not want him to be forgotten. In the beginning, I couldn't talk about him as this brought on tears. Now when the opportunity presents itself, I talk about him so much, maybe more than people care to hear. God was nudging me to find a greater purpose, because talking about him was not enough.

The impact the support group had on my life was surprising. I was not thrilled to go initially, but I found so much peace and healing with the group. I wanted to share this news with others, especially the dads. I wanted them to know about the group and have access to it. I wanted to help the dads find the courage to come and receive the same support and encouragement that I did. I figured I could be a spokesman and give a testimony or something; however, God had different plans. He didn't want me to just be a spokesman; He wanted me to lead. Tani and I soon found ourselves co-leading with Kim and then a couple of years later, leading the group on our own. In the beginning, there were many sessions where I would find myself to be the only dad among a room of grieving moms. I didn't let that discourage me and I continued to show up session after session. Eventually, my persistent presence in the group opened the doors to the men who silently carried their grief. Today, dads attending our group is part of the norm. There is no better feeling than walking alongside these moms and dads in their darkest hour and showing them love and compassion. It is no longer just helping them deal with the loss of their baby, but also strengthening the bond between couples. We always intend to bless them, but it never fails that we end up getting blessed.

Often, we tend to overlook God's calling when it makes us feel uncomfortable. For many years God has been nudging us to step out and do a little more. After much prayer and planning, we have answered

God's call and started Jake's Journey Foundation. What I have learned over the years is that words alone won't keep Jake's memory alive, but words with action make a lasting impression, bringing honor to Jake and glory to God.

Speaking of actions, I want to share a little about what it means to be angel parents to a heavenly baby. First off, we acknowledge that they exist and are counted in our family. We have pictures and mementos around the house to honor their time with us. You may get some pushback and sideways looks from others, especially when you throw your angel baby a celebration. So what? You are not living to impress others. Take some time out each year and reflect on all the blessings that have come from this short but significant life. Tani and I always attach a positive memory to Jake's heavenly birthday and will do a family outing with him. I am not saying that we don't have sad moments throughout the day, but the day as a whole is positive and cheerful.

I want to wrap up this chapter talking to the dads. There are a million different ways that your partner will want to bring honor to your child. LET HER. This is her natural motherly instinct; her need to mother her angel baby. Do not stifle it. Go with the flow, however trivial you think it is. It will mean the world to her, and it just might bring enjoyment to your life as well.

Tips for Dads:

- Acknowledge the blessings all around you. This may be as simple as getting a good parking spot at the mall or finding a ten-dollar bill in your pocket.

- God uses ordinary people to do extraordinary things. Never doubt yourself and your ability to make a difference.

- Honoring your baby can be done in many different ways—do what works for you and your partner. Remember, this is your story to write; make it remarkable.

CHAPTER SEVEN

Dear Baby

"A wife who loses a husband is called a widow. A husband who loses a wife is called a widower. A child who loses his parents is called an orphan. There is no word for a parent who loses a child. That's how awful the loss is." –Jay Neugeboren

The quote above marks the deep heartbreak of child loss. Often parents who have lost a child are referred to as a bereaved mother or father. We never cared much for the term "bereaved," we prefer the name angel mom or angel dad. Perhaps you can say there is a word for parents who lose a child, they are called "angel parents." That is how we have come to address parents, grandparents, aunts, uncles, and siblings that we have come to know in our support group.

We encourage our angel moms, dads, grandparents, and siblings to journal through their grief. It has been said that writing is therapeutic. It can trigger deep emotions and make you upset and cry, but it can also bring relief. Journaling is a major component of the support group—putting pen to paper gives all those thoughts and emotions wreaking havoc inside you a safe place to go.

This final chapter is a collection of poems and letters written by members of our support group. In reading the following pages, you will quickly realize the bond shared between a child and parent (or sibling or grandparent) is real regardless of the baby's gestational stage or age. Each shares a similar story of shattered hopes and dreams, as well as hope in God's promise for a future.

Looking back, writing these letters was not an easy task. We found it immensely difficult to articulate the love we have for our babies. We felt words could not describe the love, gratitude, disappointment, sadness, and pain that we felt inside. It took many attempts, with our eyes welled up and tears running down our cheeks, to sit down and write. We have found over the years that just like us, moms and dads would share the same struggle when writing their letter. We recall a story of a mom who pulled the blanket over her head so she could write and cry uninterrupted by her little ones. Another mom shared how she poured herself a glass of wine to get through the tears while writing her letter.

Sometimes it takes a while for us to acknowledge our loss. Sometimes we need to be told it's okay to remember and honor our baby in heaven, that it's okay to count our angel baby in our family, and that our baby's short life with us matters. It took over two years to write a letter to Baby Jul, and about four years for Baby Jo. Another mom took seven years to finally celebrate her son in heaven, while another took over twenty years. I think we all fell victim to society's lack of importance to life lost in the womb. Just like many who walk through our support group, we did not know we could remember our babies out loud.

We encourage you, if you have suffered a loss, to write to your baby, celebrate your baby, regardless of where you are in your journey or when your loss took place. It's never too late to share the life that means so much to you. This is how grandma Beatrice Friedman lovingly explained grief to her twelve-year-old granddaughter:

> *"Grief is like spilling spaghetti sauce on your favorite white blouse. You're devastated. You're thinking, how could this happen? My favorite blouse is ruined...So you go to the sink and you try to wash it out, you rub and rub and rub harder...but it's not coming out, and you cry. You think you can do without it and buy a*

new blouse, but no white shirt will do. So, you wash it some more. Over time, the spot fades...You take the white blouse out of the closet, every now and then, to see if it was just a dream, or if the spot was magically gone. And while the stain is faded even more, it's still there...While you will never forget your white blouse and the faded red stain, you have managed to live life and you will always keep the memory of the white blouse with you, always!"

You will always keep your baby's memory and the harsh sting of grief will eventually fade.

Baby Jul Leeper
8 Weeks Gestation
September 2011

Dear Baby Jul,

It took me over two years to write this letter to you. I'm sorry I didn't know then how important you are in our lives. Your presence in my belly was not planned. Your daddy and I were surprised and in tears to hear we were pregnant with you. We were unprepared but opened up to the idea of you being an addition to our family.

As quickly as you came into our lives, you were swiftly gone too. I didn't get to hear your heartbeat or have an ultrasound picture, and that saddens me. I don't know why God took you so soon. Probably you were to pave the way for us to know a love so deep that is beyond time and space.

Not knowing if you are a boy or a girl, I decided to name you Jul. I believe you were conceived in the month of July and I wanted to keep the J initial just like your dad and your brother. Thank you, my little peanut, for planting the seed in your mommy and daddy's hearts.

Until I see you in heaven.

Love,
Your Mom

Dear Baby

Baby Jo Leeper
8 Weeks Gestation
October 2015

Dear Baby Jo,

I was sad I didn't get to keep you either. Daddy and I were really hoping you were the answer to our prayers; although you were, once again it wasn't how we pictured it to be.

It took some time for me to name you and write you this letter. I am sorry. I think I quickly moved forward in trying to just accept what was. Then I realized you needed a name in heaven and people needed to know your impact in my life.

My dear baby, at the time I got pregnant with you, my interest and heart for the support group had diminished. However, God had different plans. He needed your daddy and me to continue on. He knows there are many mommies and daddies out there who need to witness His love and grace. You were the reminder that I needed to keep doing His work. It ached us to lose another baby, but your short life did not go in vain. Because of you, my passion and drive to reach and help the brokenhearted was reborn.

I have hope in knowing that one day I will get to see you and your siblings.

Love always,
Mommy

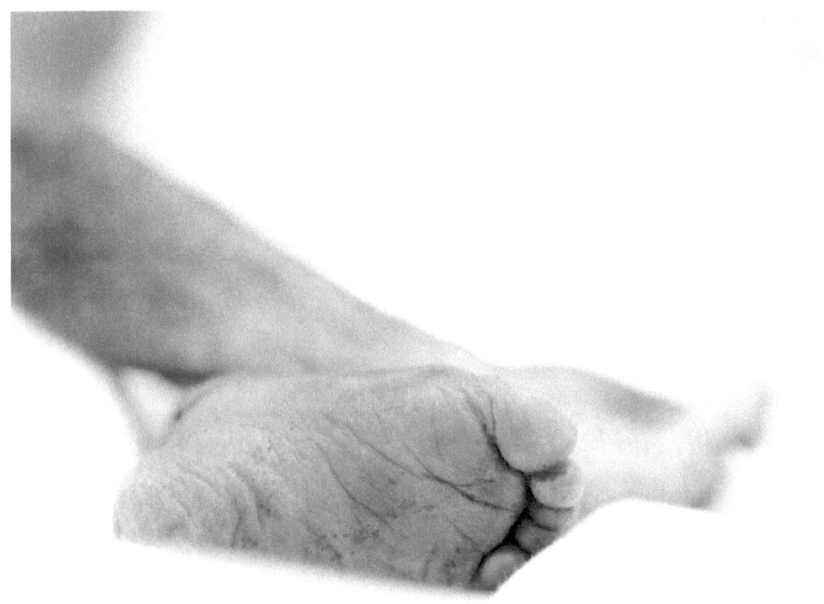

Jake Thomas Leeper
24 Weeks Gestation
January 11, 2013

My dearest baby Jake,

It has been 30 days since I last held you in my arms. Not a day goes by that I don't think of you and miss you. It's hard to put into words the deep love that I feel for you and the sorrow in knowing that I do not have the chance to raise you.

Others may find it difficult to understand my grief, for they see your time here to be so brief. What they don't understand is that I've loved and cared for you from the moment I was blessed to have you inside of me. I got to know you during the 24 weeks we spent together. I felt you move. I heard your heartbeat as you heard mine, and as my belly grew, I knew you were growing, too.

It is not fair that I don't have you here with me right now. It is not fair that I picked up your urn instead of your crib. It is not fair that I had to plan your memorial service and not your birthdays. It is not fair that I prayed for a son and now you are gone.

Your daddy and I found out the harsh reality that we would not be able to keep you on December 27th. In spite of the statistics presented to us by our honest yet sympathetic doctor, we couldn't take your life. Each time we felt your kicks and heard your strong heartbeat, we believed you were fighting to hang in there. Who are we to end a life that was so graciously given to us? Your daddy, sister, and I held tightly to the hope that you would overcome the odds.

The nurses who took care of us during our 18-day stay in the hospital were very supportive and encouraged me to hold on to hope. The early morning that you quietly came into this world on January 11th, the nurses wept. I was touched, for that meant they cared for you too.

Leaving you behind at the hospital was one of the saddest things I had to do. I wanted to take you home just like all the other mommies did with their babies. I was so sad I would never get to hold you again. Imagine my bliss when that wasn't so.

Although at the time we didn't know it, Daddy and I found the right place for you to stay until the day of your cremation. Sonya was heaven-sent. I was able to visit and spend time with you. It's funny to look back on the day when I thought if I couldn't keep you, I didn't want to see you or hold you. Forgive me for my ignorance. The eight days that I got to spend with you, holding you in my arms, were truly special and were more than I imagined I would be spending with you. I thank God for the time He allowed me to have with you. You brought joy and love to my otherwise grieving heart.

My dear son, your brief moment with us has been a blessing; you had a purpose, a reason. Your existence mended the broken pieces in my life. I truly learned of a love that is unconditional and a grief that is so profound. I discovered new heroes that I otherwise would not consider. I have a new appreciation for life and that God is truly in control of all things.

Thank you, my son, for leaving such an impression in my life. You will always be in my heart.

Love you always,
Mommy

My dear son, today we mark another milestone in our journey. I am not going to lie to you; this has been the hardest thing that I have ever had to go through. I try to be strong for Mommy but find myself breaking down when I'm alone. Oh, how I wish you were here. I wish I could hold you, and kiss you, and watch you grow. I wish I could nurture you, and guide you, and teach you all I know. I wish I could hear you cry, and watch you sleep, and feel your amazing skin. I wish things could be different. I wish I could turn back the hands of time. I wish God wouldn't have taken you from us so soon. I now must trust that He has great plans for you.

Jake, you have been a blessing to us from the start. You are a beautiful, strong, and courageous little boy. Although you never took a breath in this world, you did leave your mark on it. Everyone in this room is better today having been a part of your life. Jake, because of you, I know how it feels to love a child. I realize what a miracle each child truly is. I understand how fragile life is and that God is the one in control. I realize that you don't have to be great to have a great impact on someone's life. You have shown me that life is short, and death is for certain. You have given me a purpose to get up in the morning and continue on each day. You have brought me back to church where I find peace with God.

Jake, don't be sad for us here. We will grieve and one day be at peace. This has taught me to surround myself with people who lift me up, not bring me down. Jake, I have met many amazing individuals because of you. I have learned that asking for help is a sign of strength, not weakness. I will finish this journey that you started me on. God only knows where it will take me. One thing is for certain, it will end up with you. Until that day when we meet again, you will live in my heart.

Love,
Daddy

~

We were so happy when we found out that the kids were expecting. This would be John's first child, and we knew Tani and John would be great parents. The child would have every opportunity and a loving family. I also looked to when John would be old and have a child that would love him.

We didn't want to share the news right away, as we wanted to make sure everything would be ok. Tani, John, Tom and I would visit on the phone or in person, and we would talk about the baby. When people would ask me how they were, all I could say was, "Oh they are good." When we thought we were in the clear, it was wonderful to finally share the news with friends about Tani and John expecting a baby.

We wanted to be with the kids and part of the experience of what they were going through, as they waited for Jake to be born. We were glad we could video chat with them while they were in the hospital after Tani's water broke. The kids did everything they could to give Jake every chance to have a life.

We loved hanging out with them at the hospital. It was fun even to take a walk outside and make memories. We were all so hopeful that even when all odds were against Jake, we continued to pray and hope for a healthy baby. Shortly after Jake passed, it was hard to see other little babies and hear about other gals that were expecting. When I saw babies, I thought of Jake.

It was comforting to be allowed to be part of the process of planning the memorial service for Jake. I was so glad that we got to spend time with Jake at the mortuary; decorating his container changed the atmosphere in the room that afternoon.

Tani and John have gone to great lengths to honor Jake and keep his memory alive. I am proud of how close they are and how considerate they are of each other's feelings.

The passing of Jake has been the hardest situation I have had to accept. What I have learned is that I can do anything. Nothing is as hard as losing a child or grandchild.

It is wonderful that I have so many friends that have been a support to me and to the kids.

Jake's Grandmother

My Little Brother
by Big Sister Samantha

In anxiousness and excitement
We prepared for his arrival
But little did we know
We'd admit defeat to survival.

We tried to remain hopeful,
Even though we knew the odds.
We tried to remain strong,
But it was all up to God.

The way he fought was brave;
The way he fought was strong.
And with all the love we were prepared to give,
How could it go so wrong?

Dear Baby

I'll never get to watch him
When he starts walking to and fro.
I'll never get to support him
As he learns and grows.

I'll never get to hold him
In my arms one more time.
I'll never feel his tiny hand
As it's holding mine.

But don't think of him as tissue,
Because he was so much more.
My brother was very much alive,
Human in a tiny form.

Much like you and me,
He had a nose and feet and eyes.
We loved every inch of him,
No matter what his size.

He was much more than precious,
He was perfect in every way.
And he's never truly gone,
For in our hearts he'll stay.

Few people can understand
The sorrow that it brings,
When he was called home
And an angel gained its wings.

Michael Dexter Dominguez
38 Weeks Gestation
December 16, 2012

Dear Son,

When your mother told me we were going to have you, I was overwhelmed with happiness. Yes, yes, I did tear with joy. After we had your brother AJ, I knew all I wanted in life was to have more little ones running around. As soon as we knew you were a boy, we both wanted to name you right away. Well, to say the least, naming you became challenging. We could not agree on a name. So, the next best thing was to give you a nickname. That one was easy, my little Pac-Man.

My little Pac-Man, you grew and grew in Mommy's belly. Such an amazing miracle of life. Every day I looked forward to getting home from work just to feel you in Mommy's belly. I would talk to you endlessly. That experience is one of my fondest moments in life. I would think to myself...how much I could not wait to hold you.

Months later we had a name for you, finally. We had to compromise, of course. Mommy named you Michael and I named you Dexter. We loved your name. Our little Michael Dexter Dominguez. We were prepared for you, from your little head to your little toes. From having your little beanie, to having your little shoes, and everything in between. We prepared for months to make sure you were received with love and everything you could ever need. We were proud parents.

Dear Baby

One morning, your mommy did not feel you move like she would every morning. I was giving AJ breakfast. She came downstairs to drink cold water in the hope to have you move a little. Nothing. She then went to take a shower in another attempt to have you move. Nothing. I then realized something was wrong and went to check on her and you. She looked worried in the shower. She then told me she had not felt you that morning like she always would. I instantly started tearing, and so did she. This would turn into the worst day of my life.

Life is not always what you expect or dream. You grew your angel wings one day and life changed in a heartbeat. I struggle every day with your absence from my kisses and hugs but live-on knowing one day I will hold you and kiss you endlessly. I may never know the reason why your angel wings came early and do not expect to. All I look forward to is our family being together one day.

Know this; you have a wonderful family who cannot wait to hold you. Your older brother, AJ, has a big heart and is as intelligent as can be. Your younger sister, Kailyn, will always make you smile with her jokes and laughter. She is the sweetest little girl ever. Your mommy has so much love she wants to share with you. I am not going to lie; I may smother you constantly. Cannot wait to hold you my little Pac-Man.

Love,
Daddy

Dear Baby

Dearest Michael,

I miss you. I miss you more than words can describe. I want you to know that I'm doing ok. I'm always thinking about you. I still cry when you pop up in my head. I still feel the lump in my throat when I say your name or talk about you. I can't help but wonder who you would have grown up to be, or if you would have looked more like me than your dad.

Your sister Kailyn looks above my head and laughs sometimes. I always wondered if it was you making her laugh and smile. Your daddy broke down and cried for you this past 16th. It meant so much to me that he did that because for a long time I thought I was the only one who did. Your brother AJ asks all the time, "Where are we going?" every Sunday and says, "Oh yeah," when we say we're visiting you.

I'm sorry I don't write to you or write down my thoughts. Sometimes I just want to forget how incredibly sad I am. But there are days like today where I want to remember every thought I had of you. Your birthday is coming up, and I don't know what we're going to do. Your Lola and Papa won't be here to take another family photo. I haven't even put up the photos from your first birthday. Mommy is really lazy. That's one thing I always hoped you never got from me. Today happens to be Halloween, and I feel guilty for not decorating your plot. I hate feeling like this. I just wish you were here.

Tell God to bless me with peace. Mommy needs a lot of grace and peace in her heart. I need to let go of things and thoughts that rob me of blessings. I know you are with Jesus watching me, my little angel. I love you so much.

Behave in heaven my baby boy,
Mommy loves you

~

Dear Baby Michael,

I'm not too good at this, so it will be short and sweet. From the first time your mom told me about you, I wanted to meet you. After I met your brother and sister, I was waiting for the opportunity to visit you. When that time came, it was such an honor to do so. Even though there wasn't much talking going on, I could feel the love between you two. I felt this visit brought your mom and I even closer than we already were. The amount of love I have for your mom, brother, and sister is out of this world. They give me reason to wake up and keep going even when I feel like staying in bed all day. They give me purpose, and I promise to always take care of them to the best of my ability. As the days go by, we will continue to visit and bring flowers to you. I'm also looking forward to celebrating you later this year and the holiday photos, especially since I missed out last year while I was in Texas.

I do have one thing to ask of you, though. Please help your sister and brother come up with something to call me before Auntie Tani gets Papa Matt to stick.

*Love always and forever,
Future Stepdad*

Ayden Johnny Megas
38 Weeks Gestation, passed at 5 Days Old
April 22, 2018 – April 27, 2018

Dear Baby Boy,

I often wonder why you were chosen. So many questions and not any answers. It hurts to not have taken you outside to see the sunshine or the rain. Only God knows why; I don't understand. My beautiful baby boy, I'm sorry this happened to you. I felt so helpless. I couldn't make it better.

Every night before I sleep, I picture your big beautiful eyes and the way you looked at me. It felt amazing when I held you, played with your little hands, and kissed you so gently, and smelled your tiny feet. Although you were with us for only a few days, I'm thankful I had the opportunity to have met you. My heart is so broken. It will never be the same. Baby boy, please come into my dreams and tell me you're ok. I love you and miss you!

*Love,
Your Momma*

May 8, 2018

P.S. Today was tough knowing you will be cremated, then coming home to the mail addressed to Ayden Johnny Megas, with your social security card enclosed.

**Luke Benjamin Jones
40 Weeks Gestation
October 31, 2017**

My darling Luke,

I want to start by telling you how very loved and wanted you are and were. Your dad and I planned for you and were very excited to introduce you to your older brother, Jack, and bring you home. I am so sorry we never got to do those things. I wish more than anything I could go back in time with the knowledge I have now and figure out a way to save you. You have so many wonderful friends and family members who loved you long before you were born and were eager to meet you.

I don't understand why this happened and don't believe I ever will. It isn't right. But Dad and I have both vowed to make sure your name, memory, and legacy lives on. We are doing something charitable for you every month for the first year of your life and inviting others to join us. So far, we have adopted two sponsor children in the Dominican Republic, purchased Christmas gifts for foster children, donated supplies to the *animal shelter and donated food to the local food pantry. Even though you only lived for nine months and never got to take your first breath, you've created more good than some people do in a full lifetime. Being your parents have inspired us to be the best people we can. You sure are special, little one.*

We love you so very much, think of you every day, and never ever forget you.

Love,
Mom

Baby Kurzawinski-Propst
9 Weeks Gestation
October 21, 2018

Dear Little Peanut,

It has been almost a month since we lost you. I still miss you, do you know that? I didn't even know you and still wonder if you were a boy or a girl. Who would you have looked like? Whose personality would you have? Your hair color? So many questions left unanswered. I do know that you are someone special. You were special to me; that I will not forget!

I honestly wish that there was something I could have done differently to still have my moments with you.

Sorry, Little Peanut, for whatever reason you had to be taken from Mommy and Daddy so soon. Way too soon! We still love you and gosh, do I think about you often. My nights aren't easy when I don't have your dad by my side; I cry myself to sleep. It's not easy. But I tell myself, "One day at a time." One day we'll meet again. October 21st will now be a reason for your dad to celebrate his birthday, as we can always remember you!

You entered our lives so quickly and were taken way too quickly! You'll never be forgotten. You'll always hold a special place in my heart. Love you, and I mean it!

Love always,
Your Mommy

Four months after the first letter was written...

Dear Little Peanut,

Where does one even begin...

I fell in love with you the day I saw those two lines. I was beyond excited, shocked, surprised, and just a tad scared. I knew your dad would feel the same as I did. I still think to myself how spoiled you would be, not only by your dad and me, but by your grandparents, aunties, and your cousins, too! Still to this day I wonder if you would have been a princess or a prince? Who would you have looked like? What would your personality be like? All these questions and so many more run through my head.

I think about you every day, and I am still hurting. Why did this have to happen to you, to us??!!

I'll never get to share with you any of your first days at school, your first dance, your first date, your first birthday, first graduation, and so on. You'll always have a special place in my heart, and there's no way I will ever forget about you.

You entered all of our lives so quickly and were taken way too soon. We love you, Little Peanut. Not only will October 21st be your dad's birthday, but yours as well. We love you, and we mean it.

Love,
Mom

Zemirah Y. Amaya
18 Weeks Gestation
May 26, 2018

My dear Zemirah,

Only the heavens and God have heard me cry like a baby. My sorrow brings this misery upon me because I am missing you. Can I grieve for you forever? Will that be ok? I don't want you to think that you were something sad in my life. You were perfect, beautiful, happiness and much more. I have begged God to wake me up from this horrible dream. How can I live a happy life without you? How can this be real? Something or someone always reminds me of you. How can I ever forget about you? Some days are harder. Most days, I just want to stay in bed or drink this pain away. My showers are lonely without you, wishing you would kick my belly. It's hard to accept that my life has to go on without you when you should have been here. I miss our cuddles, Zemirah. I would do anything, and give anything, and everything, just to hold you again. Life is harder now without you. I just want you to know that I love you like God loves his son Jesus. I will hold you in my memories forever until we meet again. I will count every day to see that precious face. I love you my sweet girl.

–Mommy

Zahar Rasheed-McDuffie
30 Weeks Gestation
March 9, 2017

My beautiful angel Zahar,

Writing this is a bit challenging. I talk to you constantly but haven't written a letter to you in quite a while. Usually I write to you when I'm feeling low and sad. As I write this, I'm trying to be in good spirits which makes me feel it is unfair that I only wrote you letters in my time of angst. I'm still learning how to be a mother to you. Having an angel child is very different from having a child present here, but I always want to make sure I'm being fair and true to you.

It's been 16 months since you gained your wings. Zain and I miss you terribly, and we feel it at very different times. I always wonder what you would look like, sound like, and act like. Would you be small like Zain or chunky like your other siblings? Would you be walking by now or just starting to take steps? How many teeth would you have by now, and what foods would you like?

I miss learning your likes and dislikes, your moods and temperament. I miss those sleepless nights when you were up and moving. I miss not having sleepless nights after we separated. I miss the cries I never had the chance to hear, and the smiles I never got the chance to see. I miss the babbling and first words, the crawling and first steps. I long to express my love through hugs and kisses, helping you learn right from wrong, and picking you up when you fall and encouraging you to try again.

I really miss getting to know you. I miss the chance to be your mommy. No matter what happens, I want you to know that even though things weren't ideal, I wanted you. I love you, and nothing can replace the love I have for you. If I had to do it over again, knowing what the outcome would be, I'd do it! You are and always will be my shooting star and will always "sparkle, shine, and bloom."

—Mommy

Rebecca Grace Arevalo
24 Weeks Gestation
September 19, 2018

Dear Rebecca Grace,

Grandma's precious, precious angel. I'm writing this letter to tell you how much I love you and I will never forget the day when Mommy told me she was going to have another baby. I was so excited because I knew in my heart that you were a girl! Jacob was going to have a baby sister to love and protect. I would be at the stores waiting to buy every pink outfit, cute little ribbons for your beautiful hair, earrings, and pink Dodger outfits. We were so excited for your arrival. I remember grandpa came home with a cardboard cutout of Minnie Mouse, so I hurried up and put it away for you. I was going to spoil you rotten! Mommy and Daddy went to see the doctor to find out if you were a boy or a girl. I was right, a baby girl! But they also got the news that something was wrong. You were not doing too good, and there were a lot of things wrong. We were devastated! How could this be? I kept praying, NO they're wrong. God, please let them be wrong. We really needed a miracle. But things seemed to get worse with every visit after that. Whatever God had in store for us, we were going to love you regardless. But the odds would be against us and on September 19, 2018 God had a different plan for you. As much as we prayed and wanted you here with us, God decided he would take you instead because He didn't want you to suffer. He took you to heaven where you would be free of pain. A place where you could be happy, run, and play with all the other little angels.

Rebecca Grace, I will keep you in my heart and think of you each and every day until grandma can hold you in her arms once again. I keep the Minnie Mouse next to my angel, so I see her every morning when I wake up and every night when I go to sleep. I love you to heaven and back. Until we meet again!

Love Always,
Grandma

~

Dear Rebecca Grace,

Hello, my angel baby. I'm writing this letter to let you know I love you and you are not forgotten. I miss you so much every day. I miss feeling your precious kicks inside me as if you were dancing. It breaks my heart whenever I see a cute outfit at the store that I would have loved to dress you up in. It makes me sad that your big brother, Jacob, has no one to play with—he was so excited to meet you. You have an amazing big brother who loves you and talks about you all the time. You guys would have had a great bond. You may not know this, but your lil' life has touched a lot of people, and we pray for you every day. I was so happy to find out you were a girl, and I was ready to take you on trips to the nail salon and style your hair so pretty. Your dad was excited to throw you a quinceañera; I know he's crazy, but that's your dad. I think about you every day and I wish I could hold you in my arms again. I just didn't want to let you go.

Saying goodbye to you was the hardest thing I had to do. Until we meet again my sweet girl, what better place to meet than heaven. I know you're in good hands with plenty of family and friends by your side and always watching over us, waiting for us at those heavenly gates. I always think of you whenever I see a beautiful butterfly. It's hard to take flowers to your grave because I see you're not alone, you're with all the other babies that are gone too soon. I try not to cry too much, but I can't help it. I miss you. Then when I see the beauty of where you are, I can't help but think how lucky you are, and you can fly. How cool must it be to have Jesus bouncing you on his knee and playing peek-a-boo with you. I'll see you again one day my lil' angel in heaven. Mommy loves you so much, more than you'll ever know.

Love,
Mommy

Koa Aiken
11 Weeks Gestation
December 1, 2019

Baby Koa,

Mommy loves you more than you could ever know. Me and Daddy are so blessed that God gave us you. I know you are the most amazing, brave, God-fearing little one. In your short time here with me, you helped Mommy make sense of so many things I never thought I could understand. I often wonder what your precious face looks like; if you have Daddy's dimples. I picture your sweet innocent smile as I write this and don't even know how. You, my baby, make me a mommy, the one thing I have always longed for. You have brought me so much happiness that I can't even explain. How do I love someone so much that I haven't even met yet? God gave us you for a reason. Although I may have some hard days and weak moments, Koa you make Mommy so much stronger and continue to make me stronger every single day. The love that I have for you is infinite. You are my sun, my smile, and the air that I breathe. My hope, my joy, you make me brave. I can't wait to bring your siblings into the world for you to watch over. I do believe that after every storm comes a rainbow, but Koa you were never a storm. You were that happy long-awaited raindrop that brings so much happiness after a drought. You are the flower we see sprout and bloom after waiting and wondering if we watered too much or too little. You are and always will be Mommy's "why." Thank you for choosing me to be your mommy, Koa. I know it is true that "every good and perfect gift is from above, coming down from the Father of the heavenly lights, who does not change like shifting shadows," (James 1:17).

Mommy loves you. Please don't drive our dog, Baby, too crazy up there, and I hope you enjoy your Mema's French fries up there. Your daddy loves you so much.

> "I prayed for this child, and the Lord has granted me what I asked of Him. So now I give him to the Lord. For his whole life he will be given over to the Lord," (1 Samuel 1:27-28).
>
> *–Mommy*

Chavez Babies
5 Weeks Gestation | 7 Weeks Gestation Twins | 7 Weeks Gestation
March 5, 2018 | July 4, 2018 | April 16, 2019

To my beloved baby quartet (BBQ),

I miss what could have been.

Although we've never met, just know that I love you with all of my heart. I always wonder if you will have your mom's smile or your dad's eyes. Wondering saddens me though because it's not reality. You are never forgotten, my quartet. Nobody did anything wrong. Your grandpa says, "Sometimes we don't know why these things happen." I'll take care of your mom down here and watch over us up there. Don't forget to kiss your mom every night before she goes to bed. I love your mom with everything that I am, as I do you my quartet.

I see and feel all four of you just a little older and hanging on me with two at my legs, one on my arm and the other around my neck—smiling and laughing. When the time comes, we will be united.

With all my love,
Your Pop

Xavier "Xavi" Gregory Jabonillo
40 Weeks Gestation, passed at 20 Hours Old
February 9, 2019 – February 10, 2019

Dear Xavi,

My son…I miss and love you beyond words and life itself. I know you are in the best place, especially after my recent dream of you and Tatay (Grandpa) together. I know you two are having the best time. Please watch over your mommy and daddy, Xavi, as we go through our first holidays without you. We wanted to take you to see Candy Cane Lane, take your first pictures with Santa for our Christmas card, celebrate my birthday and say, "I do not need anything because I have Daddy and you." I want to feel your heavy weight at nine months old, I want to keep breastfeeding you for at least one year. I want to watch holiday movies with you and think life is perfect because I have everything I need right here.

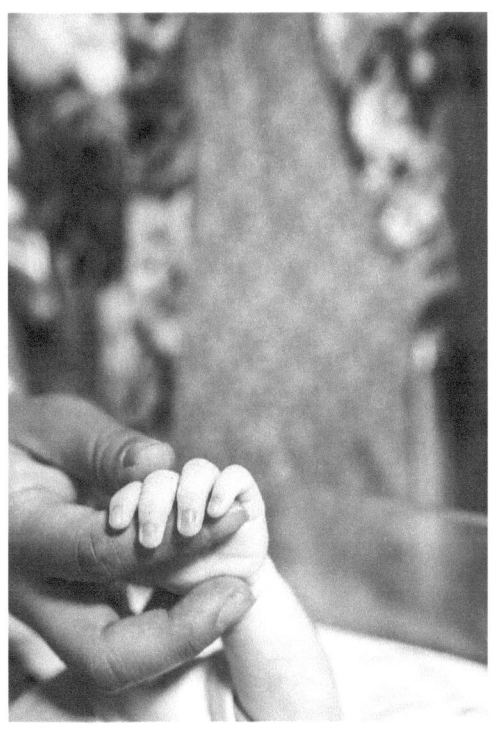

Xavi, please ask Jesus to have mercy on us and help heal us, ok baby? Be our strongest prayer warrior because we need it. Love you to the heavens and back my beautiful son.

Your Mommy

~

My son. We're coming up to a year since you left us. Your mom and I miss you so much. Halloween was very difficult, and the anticipation of the upcoming holidays gives us anxiety. Only if you were here. Please continue to visit both of us, especially your mom. We anticipate every hummingbird, or any moment that resembles hope, love, and peace; but what we anticipate more is the day we can hold you again. You're our future my son. Pray that your mom and I have the courage, strength, and peace to get through the tough days and to make you proud.

Love and miss you,
Your Dad

Vinny Inez
6 Weeks Gestation
June 20, 2019

Dear Baby V,

I wish I could have held you in my arms, but really, I wish I had more time with you. I want you to know the moment I found out that we were blessed with you, I loved you with all my heart! I planned on teaching you so many things and spending all my time with you. Showing you how to work on cars, going to the shooting range, and teaching you all the things my father passed on to me. Every day I think about you and how I wish things were different, but I want you to know that you are well taken care of up there with God. Trust in Him even though I'm mad at Him. I know God will help you grow and show you how to heal me.

I love you,
Dad

~

Dear Nugget,

Mommy sat down to write to you, and I just went on and on about all the things I missed and all the things I hoped for you and our little family. Like watching you grow and learn from Daddy and watching you be Daddy's little helper around the house and with the cars. Mommy could just picture you running and waddling to Daddy to hand him a tool and giggling as you ran back to me. I was so excited to see you play and become best friends with your big furry brother. I know you both would tire each other out and I'd catch you both snuggling during nap time. And because you're my wild child, I know I'd find you two napping in Blue's bed and not yours. You and Blue would be my little troublemakers, but it would make for the best memories. Most of all I was so eager to see just how much of a smarty pants you'd grow up to be. Daddy and I were so excited to have a mini us. I simultaneously dreaded and longed for the days that would come when we'd laugh until we cried because you and Daddy would be cracking jokes at Mommy's expense. It makes me a little happy that grandma and great grandpa are in heaven with you. It means you'll still be exposed to Daddy's sarcasm and Mommy's quick one-liners. After all, that's who we learned from.

My little love, of all the things I wrote down, the most important thing I want you to know is that Mommy and Daddy love you so, so much. Our love for you has been growing in our hearts long before we knew you. We wanted you more than anything in the world. We still do, and it's so hard to accept that we don't get to have you. To hold you, to kiss you, to tuck you into bed. To tell you we love you and to hear you say it back. The holidays are coming, and I'm worried we won't enjoy them. Every special event now feels so empty. All I can think is you should physically be here with us during these moments. I'm so worried it's always going to feel this way, but I promise I'll try to enjoy these things for you. Tell grandma "Hi" for me and if heaven has TV, ask her to make sure you know all about The Rugrats. Even better, maybe you can come and visit me in my dreams, and we can watch them together. I will love and miss you forever, my little angel.

Love,
Mommy

Seven months after the first letter was written...

Dear Vinny,

These past 9 months have been the most heartbreaking 239 days of my life. But that will never take away that you, my big love, are the reason Mommy also got to experience the absolute best 13 days of her life!

Yesterday was your due date. Valentine's Day. So fitting for our little love child. Yesterday could have been the day I got to meet you, to lay my eyes on you, study you, breathe in your scent and plant loving kisses on your head. As much as I would have loved for yesterday to be that day, it just isn't time for us to meet yet. I don't fully understand that notion, but I am learning to accept it.

My little angel yesterday was the ending to a painful chapter in our lives. It's now time for Mommy to let you go; to not hold you down here on earth and in my mind, but to let you fly freely. Do not worry about your mommy and daddy being sad. By letting go, I do not mean that there will ever be a day that passes that we won't miss you, or think about you, or never talk about you. But it means letting go of thinking of you as who you should have been and beginning to see you as who you are. I know I cannot know physical traits just yet, but I do believe I know your soul. Your gentle, loving, and a little smart-butty soul. I know this because God made you in His image (and a little of Mommy and Daddy's image, too). Our God is a loving and gentle God. He is also a forgiving God. Mommy hasn't had the best attitude with Him lately, but I know He won't give up on me. Please let Him know I'm sorry and I'm trying to do better.

It's time for Mommy to fully let go. You see my love, I think that's the only way you're going to be able to make your way into my arms. I know when you help God send your sibling down to earth, a little bit of you will come with him or her. That makes Mommy so hopeful and happy. I do hope and pray that every once in a while, God lets you come and visit Mommy and Daddy in our dreams. I would love to spend some time with you. Oh, and thank you for my teddy bear, love. It made Mommy's day yesterday.

My love, thank you for giving Mommy life again. For bringing us a sign of hope. For setting us on this path to reunite us with God. Mommy will always miss you, my first born. Enjoy your peace in heaven my little angel.

God has you in heaven, but I have you in my heart, always!

Love,
Mommy

Baby Gutierrez
9 Weeks Gestation
October 2019

Dear Baby G,

I think about you all the time, and often wonder who you would have looked like and what kind of personality you would have. I think of all the holidays and big moments we would have with you by our side and in our arms. I think about how much love you would have had around you because we've got a butt-load of amazing family and friends who would spoil you rotten.

Unfortunately, you were taken too soon for reasons we will never know until we meet again. My heart breaks knowing you couldn't see the joy on your mom and dad's face when you first enter their world, or hear my favorite music play, or hear me play guitar for you. It breaks my heart knowing you never felt the sun on your face, or saw snow fall in my hometown in New Mexico, or got kisses from your father's lips—he has the best lips to get kisses from—or met your big sister. She would've loved to hold you any second your father and I weren't holding you, and play with you. You would've loved to meet your grandparents, great grandparents, and everyone else in our great big family. I am hopeful we will all be reunited in God's Kingdom one day and everything will all make sense. Till then angel baby G, we will always and forever love you.

Love,
Mama

Gabriel Joseph Alviar
32 Weeks Gestation
February 12, 1998

Today I rejoice! Today you would've turned 21 years old. Today brings so many "what-ifs" in my mind and thoughts of memories and milestones never made. Through this I learned that grieving for you will not end in this lifetime. That the empty space will never be filled. That it's still painful to think of you. I loved you the moment I found out about you. A kind of love I never thought possible. Time and absence have not changed that, it is stronger than ever. My heart is heavy, but today I rejoice. Even though we are not together, because of you, I know love never dies! See you in heaven my dear son! Because of this great pain, I know I will have great joy when I finally hold you in my arms!

Love,
Mommy

Ainsley Logan Chambers
15 Weeks Gestation
November 19, 2019

Dear Ainsley,

Mommy loves you and misses you every day. I miss feeling you move inside me. I hope you know just how wanted and loved you are. I hope you know that I tried my best to keep you safe. I hope that you can feel our love for you, and I hope you are surrounded by your Great Grandma Jo, Great Grandpa George, and the rest of our family. My arms ache to hold you. I want you to know that while I pray that Daddy and I are blessed with another child, your new sibling could never and would never replace you. You will forever hold a piece of my heart, just as your sister, Audrey, holds a piece of my heart. I pray that you felt no pain when you gained your wings, and you only felt the love that we have for you. I want you to know how sorry I am that I don't get to hold you and watch you grow. I feel like I failed you in some way, and I am sorry for that too. Please watch over your sister and your brother and help keep them safe. If you meet our little embryo, please tell him or her that Mommy loves him or her, too.

With all my heart,
Mommy

Evan Maldonado
32 Weeks Gestation
December 15, 2018

Dear Baby Evan,

What can I say, my dear baby, that you haven't already heard from me? I'm so thankful and blessed to be your mom. I cherished the time I was able to carry you and hold you finally in my arms. You don't know how much you have touched our lives. I think about you constantly, baby boy. I know you are at peace resting in heaven with Ma and sitting next to our Lord waiting for us. You touched so many lives in the little time you were here. I know your life has a purpose. I promise to honor your name as long as I am here on this Earth. Your story will be told over and over until I am no longer. My sweet baby boy, your brother, Dylan, misses you and talks about you often. I know you don't need to be here physically for him to play with you, but it would've been nice. We know of God's promises and wholeheartedly trust we will all unite one day. There are times we are sad and there are times we still wonder how you would look as a grown boy, but we know you will always be the center of an untold story where pain creeps in and out from time to time. We know to follow in faith, allow our hearts to be filled more with God's love, and draw us nearer while the pain subsides. We will continue on so your story will be able to draw unbelievers closer to our merciful God. Thank you, baby Evan, for allowing me to be your mom and to share your story. I will love you always until the day we will surely meet again.

Your proud Mommy

Stella Rose Espinoza
40 Weeks Gestation, passed at 15 Days Old
January 27, 2019 – February 11, 2019

To my beautiful Stella,

Day after day I've thought of what I'd want to write to you that I haven't said to you every time I visit your grave or as I'm cleaning and reorganizing your things. But one thing I don't think I've said is, "Thank you." Thank you for choosing *me to be your mommy, for allowing me to meet you, and for making me a stronger person. The day I lost you, as Daddy and I walked out of the hospital with an empty car seat, I wanted my life to end as well. I wanted to join you and hold you in my arms forever, but you and God had a different plan for me; you held my hand as I continued to survive without half of my heart. I also thank you for leaving your daddy with me because in him I see you. No matter how much I'd complain every time I hear that you are his twin, I must agree. You have his smile, you slept like him, and when you'd have your bath, you would get those curly, curly curls just like him. Thank you, baby, for wanting to sleep only in my arms that last night we had with you. I didn't understand why you only wanted to sleep when I'd lay you on my chest, but now I know you were saying goodbye. I hope that as I'm writing this letter you are looking over me, missing me as much as I miss you. I miss you more than words will ever be able to explain, and even though you gained your wings, my love for you will continue to grow. I hope we get to see you again, and that you are the one who welcomes me into heaven along with your baby brother or sister that Daddy and I didn't get to meet. Please tell him or her I am so sorry. I'm sorry I was scared, too scared of losing again, that I couldn't be 100% excited. But my heart broke into a billion pieces all over again the day the doctor said there was no heartbeat. I felt as if I was watching your heart stop on that monitor all over again. I promise to be brave next time if I get the chance to be a mommy again. I promise to love and cherish my pregnancy and our baby the way I did with you, Stella. I love you, and there is not a day that goes by when I don't miss you and wish you were here with us as we watch you grow. I love you, Stella Rose.*

Love,
Mommy

Noah Sebastian Godinez | Lorenza Josefina Godinez | Scarlett Love Godinez
10 Weeks Gestation | 12 Weeks Gestation | 7 Weeks Gestation
February 3, 2011 | February 18, 2011 | November 10, 2019

A Father in Grief

F – frightened for my wife
A – afraid of not making the right decisions
T – tormented by the thought of losing a wife and child
H – hurt from my heart almost pumping out of my chest
E – escape; trying to find a way out of this situation
R – rage for this happening

I – impatient at the ambulance not getting to our house in time
N – nights; the long nights we stayed up in the hospital

G – God; I prayed to not take my wife and child away
R – rescue for emergency surgery by Dr. Nauizade
I – illuminating; for the knowledge our doctor had to do the surgery

E – emotional roller coaster we went through
F – faith in God for hearing my prayers

Grief

G – grief; the mental distress of our loss
R – remorse; not knowing if we did something wrong
I – incapable; not able to help my wife with her pain
E – ending; having to end our child's life
F – faith; God will give us a baby one day

MaryGrace Hope Pearson
15 Weeks Gestation
January 15, 2020

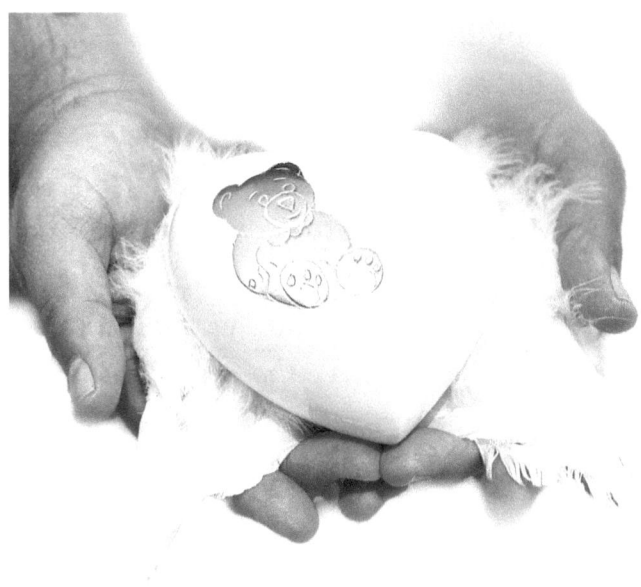

Sweet MaryGrace,

I have been writing "the story of you." It's been tough, but I need to do this, not only for me but also because I need you to know how much we fought for you. Your big sister, Faith, is taking care of you every chance she can, from praying for you every day and keeping your candle lit, to insisting we take your urn with us camping to make sure your candle never goes dark. Faith said you would have gone on future camping trips with us had you not left us so soon, so taking your urn is you coming along.

I long to hold you in my arms, and while I know I will someday, I wish that someday was today. Every day I look at the calendar and think about what life would be like, today, with you in our lives. We would have brought you home around your original due date, July 8th. I planned to be off of work until November. Faithyyy wasn't going to camp so we could spend the summer bonding; the three girls in the house. We planned to help you with tummy time together. Faith was even getting into the idea of changing your diaper. We were excited to dip your toes into the water for the first time. I wonder if you would have liked the water like Faithyyy and Daddy do. We planned to take you to Leo Carrillo State Park. We thought it would be fun to take pictures since you were in my tummy when we had our family pictures done there. I remember that day; we had so much fun. We weren't ready to tell anyone about you yet. You were our happy little secret, and we giggled knowing that we had a secret. Would you have liked the ocean? The *feeling of the sand between your toes? I love the ocean; I feel so relaxed at the beach. We have all the plans, all the wonders, and sometimes it helps for me to create a vision for myself that answers my wonders.*

I know you have made the sweetest friends in heaven. I am sure by now you have made best friends with Ainsley, and met Vinny, who you and your friends try to keep out of trouble. I am sure Jake shows you all the cool things to play with. Is it like a heavenly summer camp for babies?

I know Grandpa Howie, Grandma Bubbles, Grandpa Max, and Great Grandma Nellie are looking after you and loving on you. I am jealous, I wish I could love on you. Someday...I will need to write to you about wooden nickels, paper dimes, and clean eyeballs, so you can play those games with Grandpa Howie.

I miss my Daddy. You're in really good hands.

"I'll love you forever, I'll like you for always" (Robert N. Munsch).

You Are My I Love You. I will love you for eternity.

Love,
Mommy

Victoria Genesis Herrarte
18 Weeks Gestation
March 31, 2020

Dear Baby,

Even though we have never met in person, I will always love you. I don't know what type of child or person you would have become, but if it's anything like your brother and sisters, you would have been a wild one. I know it's not your time to be born, and that you're with God now, but I will also love you and miss you for the rest of my life until I get to see you.

I can imagine you looking down on us seeing all of the crazy things your brother and sisters do, as well as your mom and dad, and just saying, "These people are crazy." I can imagine your laughs, smiles, and cries. I didn't like being in the hospital with you and not hearing any noise, that was one of the worst experiences ever. I wish never to relive that again.

I hope you're saying good things about your family in heaven because one day I'll meet you in person and give you the biggest hug ever.

I miss you,
Your Dad

Dear Victoria,

I want to start by telling you how much I miss you and wish you could still be with us. I know you are with God and you are having the best time of your life up in Heaven. You probably met your three cousins. I hope you guys are having fun together. My heart aches because I don't have you growing in my stomach and feeling you move when I would put worship music on for you. I know you are worshiping God right now in heaven. Please know that I will always love you, and you will always be a part of our family; even when others consider you to be no more than a fetus. You were always more than that; you were our little girl and I will always have that picture of holding you and telling you how much I love you and always will.

Love,
Mom

Bailey Castillo
12 Weeks Gestation
May 7, 2020

Dear Bailey,

Mommy and Daddy miss you very much. We wish you were here with us counting down the days when we would've gotten the chance to hold you in our arms. From the day we found out we were expecting you, you were mommy's best friend. No symptoms, from day one. On the other hand, Daddy was the one feeling light-headed, getting nausea, and was always craving something new. It was very fun getting to watch what you put Daddy through.

From the moment we found out, Mommy had already picked out a Disney outfit for you to come home in. We knew you were going to love Disneyland as much as we do! We were already thinking of getting your annual pass!

Although we were not able to keep you, the world had other plans for you. We can tell right now that you are probably in heaven giggling, smiling, and making peoples' day with just your smile.

You are probably playing with your great grandma and great grandpa. Enjoying the nice weather in Mexico heaven. We know for a fact that Daddy's grandparents are taking very good care of you.

We came up with a name for you, although we do not know your gender. Your name will always be Bailey Castillo to us. We both got a tattoo of a heartbeat symbolizing you since that was the closest we got to be to you.

Every morning Daddy would kiss you before he left to work. When Sebas woke up he would always do the same. Every night big brother would say he wanted two girls and one boy. We think he is getting tired of being the only child. He couldn't wait to meet you and be the best big brother and role model to you.

Love,
Mommy and Daddy

Flores Twins	**Heavens Angel Flores**
4 Weeks Gestation	15 Weeks Gestation
February 2015	October 20, 2019

I'm going through all my wishes right now. Wishing I was hearing you all laugh. Wishing I was seeing the beautiful smiles. Wishing I could hear the cries just so I can find a way to make you all happy. Wishing you were all here so I can spend time with you. Wishing you were here with me on Father's Day. My twins and my princess, I love you. On a day where I thought I would wake up feeling alone, thank you for sending all your love to me from the Heavens above. I have you three always looking down, watching me raise Abel, Eli, and Allyson, knowing I'm not a stepfather but a father. Please God give me the patience to be the best father possible here on earth. God has a purpose for me. I know one day I'm going to be reunited with you, my twins and my princess, in the kingdom of heaven. Daddy just has to do his part and complete his purpose! Easier said than done. I miss you still my babies, always my babies, my beautiful children I love you.

–Daddy

Bernas Babies
8 Weeks Gestation - 14 Weeks Gestation
Dates Undisclosed

Dear Angel Babies,

We wish you were here for us to hold. We wish we could see you laugh and play with Victoria and Little Kenny, but we know you are all in heaven looking out for us. When we see your siblings, we wonder what similarities you all might have. We wonder if Victoria is a combination of all of you. We wanted all of you so bad and were in so much pain when we lost you. We prayed for you and when we couldn't hold you, we cried. We think about you often. We see you in the flowers, we see you in the sky and morning sun, and we see you in the eyes and smiles of your sister and brother.

Sidney – 9 Weeks Gestation
When we went to the doctor, we did not hear your heartbeat. A few days later you were gone. Your daddy and I named you Sidney. We grieve you even up to this day, our angel in heaven. We long for the day when we get the privilege to hold you in our arms for the first time, to kiss your face, to smell your scent, to call you by your name, "Our Sidney, our sweet, sweet, Sidney."

Tiffany – 12 Weeks Gestation
We never got to feel you, but we did get to see you. You were smaller than the palm of our hands. You were still in your baby sack and with a splash we knew you were gone. Our baby doll,

our middle child, like a Tiffany necklace, we hold you forever close to our hearts.

Daisy – 10 Weeks Gestation

A baby on the way, that's what the test said. We bought you your first dress at a store called Pumpkin Patch. We wouldn't lose you. You were going to make it, was what we thought. But you never got to wear your Pumpkin Patch dress, so tiny and decorated with flowers. Our Daisy, so delicate and fragile, yet the tormenting pains mom had that night we will never forget. There was screaming and groaning in the bathroom, trying to silence myself so daddy wouldn't hear me. Mommy didn't want to scare him. Mommy's tears flowed at night when the whole world slept. Not a soul could feel mommy's pain. Mommy's tears could have watered an entire garden full of daisies, roses, and lilies. Little did we know our journey wasn't over, more tears were destined to flow.

Lily – 14 Weeks Gestation

You were the strongest. You made it to 14 weeks. We could feel the excitement, but then it all changed. As quickly as you came into our lives you were gone, like our other babies. The doctor said that you were a girl; we knew it. Although you were with us on earth for only a short time, we knew you, mommy had felt you, we had seen you in our dreams and we still do.

Rose – 8 Weeks Gestation

Mommy had you in my tummy the shortest amount of time. We were so excited to see a positive mark on my test. You are the reason our story changed. After you, we felt like we couldn't continue this battle alone. We've heard a lot of people talk about miracles, but they're hard to believe unless they happen to you. We surrendered our struggle to God and when we did, He blessed us with our first full term baby, your sister Victoria. We never got to hold you, but we know that there is a piece of each of our angel babies in your sister and brother.

Love,
Mommy and Daddy

Jeremiah Wynott
13 Weeks Gestation
January 13, 2012

Dear Baby,

I'm writing you a letter you will never read. As difficult as this is, the need for me to express my love for you far exceeds the need to push this pain away. It all happened so fast; I'm still trying to wrap my mind around it.

January 13, 2012, 5:00 p.m. I got up from resting to use the bathroom. I had been having some slight stomach cramps throughout the day, so I thought I'd lay down for a bit. While peeing, I felt something pass through me. It wasn't painful, but I knew it wasn't right. "Please God, NO," I remember saying as I reached for the light. I turned to see two drops of blood on the floor, and my heart fell. Realizing that gravity was not my friend right now, my first instinct was to lay on my bed.

Your daddy and oldest brother, Blake, were at soccer practice. Thankfully, your 12-year-old brother, Ryan, was in his room and came running as soon as I called his name. "Ry, something's wrong, I need you to grab my cell phone so that I can call the doctor."

Now, 5:08, the doctor was gone, but the service assured me she would call me back. I hung up and asked Ryan if he would please pray, for I could not. "Dear, Lord..." then the phone rang. Dr. Silberstein assured me that cramping and spotting were normal in the first trimester (even though I was in my second). As for the feeling of something passing through me— that she could not explain—when I got off the phone, I knew I would have to investigate. Ryan got me a towel as I returned to the bathroom. I told him I had no idea what I was about to pull out of there and if he wanted to leave, I would completely understand.

"I'm staying," came his unwavering answer.

I reached to the back of the toilet with strength that was not my own. The next thing I remember is opening my hand to see you for the first time. A perfectly intact 13-week-old fetus. I was shocked.

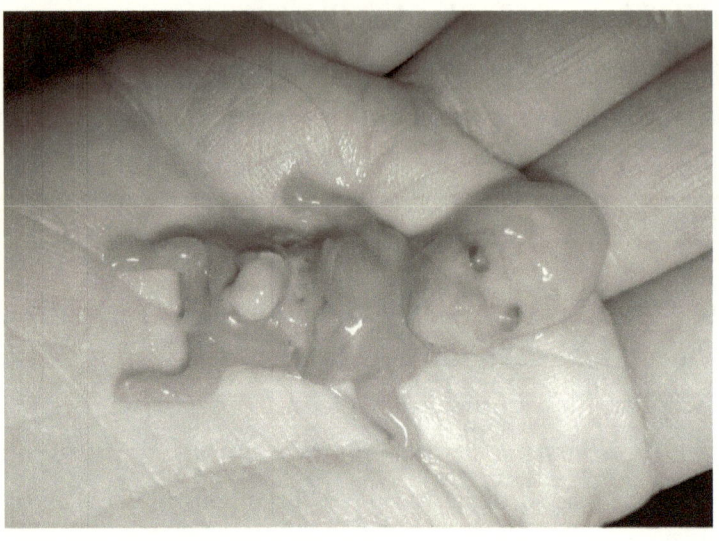

"That's our baby", Ryan blurted.

We stood there just staring at you in disbelief. Your eyes were the bluest eyes I'd ever seen. There were your legs and arms; I could even count your fingers and toes. And from what I could tell, the boys would have gotten their wish for another brother. You seemed to have all that you needed. Why are you here so soon—too soon?

I pushed re-dial on the phone and told my doctor what I held in my hand. She, of course, was so sorry for my loss, but so surprised at the way it happened. Most miscarriages are not that clean and few ever allow you to hold your baby, well at least not at 13 weeks.

I got off the phone and told Ryan that for some reason this baby was needed more in heaven than it was on earth. Most of the time, your brother, Ryan, has maturity beyond his years that I find a little scary, but days like today, it clearly is a gift and a blessing. He calmly said, "Things happen for a reason," and with that, he hugged me, I mean he really hugged me.

We put you in a small glass bowl with some water so that Daddy and Blake could see you and say good-bye to you. Ryan went off to his room for some alone time. Unable to get a hold of your dad earlier, he called me back to see what was up. Your conception was a bit of a surprise, but your untimely birth was a shock neither of us were prepared for. He kept saying, "I am so sorry." After 18 years of marriage, I knew he meant he was sorry for all of us. For the last three months, the four of us would grow more and more excited each day. We bonded as a family discussing your development, your gender, and your possible name. We were so excited when we could finally send your picture through emails, texts, and Facebook to let all our friends and family know of our uncontainable joy. Now, within only seconds, it was being taken away from us.

I got off the phone, and in God's perfect timing, began going through the process of delivering the sack and all that comes with the miracle of birth. This was the step my doctor couldn't explain me skipping. But right then I knew…God gave me not only the opportunity to hold my baby, completely intact, without distraction or pain, but he waited on "the yucky stuff." He is a just God, despite my grim situation.

By the time your dad and Blake walked through the door, the reality of it all had set in. Ryan came out of his room and shared our sad news with Blake. The two of them are so different. Blake, so much like your dad, not quite sure how to give in to his emotions; needing extra time to walk away and process things. This worked out well, for Ryan and I had shared all the words we needed. Now we all just shared understanding looks of heartbreak and the comfort that can only come from the hug of someone who is feeling your same pain.

They saw you, were amazed by you, and then couldn't look anymore. Ryan and I kept coming back to you, learning something new that we hadn't seen before, etching you in our memory. But we all deal with grief differently, and that's perfectly okay.

I took a photo of you. It seemed strange to want to capture the moment. But I somehow had such a peace, and I knew God was going to reveal things to me over time. Anyway, I didn't find you gross and unfinished. Honestly, you were one of the most precious things I had ever seen. Seeing you made it real to me, to us, and I knew there were lots of others out there who also had fallen in love with the idea of you. It might help them say good-bye as well.

Before I let you go, I want to tell you that your life was not a waste. I am certain there are moments to come, lives that will be touched, and miracles we may never know about. I am proud to be your mom and honored to have been able to hold *you for a brief moment here on earth. I will always remember January 13 as the day you came into the world and changed my life forever. This will not be known as the date that I lost you, rather, the date that I glimpsed at eternity and felt the hand of God upon me.*

So, goodbye my sweet baby, but just for a while. I know with great certainty that I will see you again. And I know until that day—you will be in the best of hands.

I love you,
Mommy

**To read more of these beautiful letters
visit our website at**
https://jakesjourney.org/dear-baby-letters

About The Authors

Tani DeGuzman Leeper was born and raised in Manila, Philippines. At the age of 14, she, her mother, and two sisters moved to sunny California. Life was average as she recalls it. After graduating from high school, she attended a local community college while working three jobs to purchase her first car.

When she was 19 years old, she became pregnant with her daughter, Samantha. Her family demanded that she get an abortion. When she refused, her family disowned her. She immediately found herself homeless, living out of her car, going from motel to motel, and trying to figure out what's next. Losing her immediate family hurt her deeply, but killing her baby was not an option. Even at a young age, she knew the sanctity and precious gift of life in the womb.

She married Samantha's dad, but later divorced. They maintained an amicable relationship and prioritized Samantha's well-being beyond their own. Determined to finish college, she went back to school and graduated Cum Laude with a Bachelor of Science degree in Child and Adolescent Development from California State University, Northridge. She worked at several elementary schools as a primary educator for 18 years.

In her early thirties, she remarried. She and her husband, John, hoped to have a child of their own. Their hopes resulted in multiple losses. Knowing the pain of pregnancy loss too well, and the faith that drove them out of the darkness, it became their mission to walk alongside moms and dads during their time of grief.

As a team, Tani and John lead In Loving Arms pregnancy loss support group and are co-founders of Jake's Journey Foundation, where they help provide financial assistance towards burial or cremation services for babies lost through stillbirth or neonatal loss. Through their story they hope to change how society approaches life lost in the womb. They want to spread understanding and compassion that when a parent suffers a loss, it is not a tissue, it is their baby. A baby they loved and hoped for. A life they imagined that abruptly ended.

Tani's favorite activity is spending time with her husband and daughter. She finds joy in the simplest things that they do together—sitting around the dinner table, evening walks with their dog Rylee, or spending time in the water. She dreams of one day spending more time traveling with them, learning about the rich history of our beautiful world. Together they care for Tani's mother, who lives with them, in beautiful Simi Valley, CA.

tani@jakesjourney.org
jakesjourney.org

John Leeper was born and raised in the San Francisco Bay Area. John has always loved the water and boating, from outings on the boat with his family as a young boy, to working at a boat shop after school for extra cash. John attended California State University, Hayward and received a Bachelor of Science degree in Business Administration and Computer Information Systems. He did not work in that field a day in his life, as the call of the water was louder. He pursued his passion as a boat technician and became the best in his field.

In May 2002, not long after his divorce, John met the love of his life, Tani. In January 2003, he packed up his house and moved to Southern California to build a life with her. Seven months later, they were married. In 2008, during the market crash, the company he was working for closed its doors. He saw this as an opportunity to start JTS Marine Inc., and a thriving boat service and repair business was born.

John helped raise and care for Tani's daughter Samantha, but he realized he wanted to have a child of his own, their "us baby" as a friend lovingly terms it. Their dreams were crushed after three pregnancies in a five-year span ended in two miscarriages and one stillborn son. John picked up the pieces and adopted a passion to serve the bereaved community.

From their losses, John and Tani lead In Loving Arms support group, where he does an amazing job presenting the male

perspective on grief and loss. He helps to give a voice to the men in the group and make them feel safe and comfortable to share their feelings. John's involvement in the group also helps moms gain perspective on how the dads might be feeling, which opens up the communication on grief.

In true partnership, John and Tani have successfully continued to build from brokenness. They found a calling in giving back and helping others who face similar struggles and founded Jake's Journey Foundation. Through their foundation, they are making a tangible difference in the community. It has become their lifework to change the way the world views life lost in the womb.

John is a man of simple pleasures—spending time with his wife, whether out on the open water or lounging in the pool, watching sports with his stepdaughter, and grilling up some good meat are his ideas of a good time.

john@jakesjourney.org
jakesjourney.org

Acknowledgements

"Writing a book was the domain of Harvard graduates, academics, and the entrepreneurs that were ahead of the curve." –Natasa Denman

For someone who does not fall in any of those categories, I never imagined I would be joining the ranks of published authors. When I first embarked on this journey, I was not sure how it would all work out. Turning an idea into a book is not as easy as one would think; however, more rewarding than one could imagine. This book is a labor of love.

To my husband, best friend, and number one fan, John, thank you for always believing in me when I sometimes do not even believe in myself. For being patient with me when the days were long and rough. For burning the midnight oil with me, writing, and editing, without complaint, even after you had a lengthy day at work. You will forever be my best "Hi." I love you more than words can express.

To my talented and awesome daughter, Samantha, thank you for reading my first drafts and helping me with the countless revisions and edits. For putting up with me when I was feeling frustrated. For rooting me on when I felt discouraged. For picking up the slack at home when I was too busy writing. You are just as much a part of this book and a vital component in getting me to where I am today. I would choose you all over again. I love you to the moon and back.

To my friend Kim Preston, I am eternally grateful for your courage to start a support group. Thank you for walking alongside me and John during the darkest time of our life and for gently teaching me about a relationship with God, which led my family back to church. I am honored to be growing the seed you planted.

To my friend and fellow angel momma, Gladys P. Jabonillo, thank you for helping get the chaos in my head onto paper and executing a systematic plan. For reading, or should I say dissecting, my first chapters which helped tremendously in guiding my writing. For the weekly "Boss Lady" meetings to make sure I was staying on task and giving me much-needed encouragement.

Acknowledgements

To my friend, Mari Orosa, thank you for your willingness to read my manuscript and sharing your constructive feedback, comments, and criticisms. I cherish your friendship and respect your honesty and wisdom.

To my once kindergarten student and now friend, Isabella McDonald-Brent, thank you for your critique and feedback during the last haul of this journey. For looking up to me and cheering me on along the way. To think I once taught you how to construct your first sentence, and now you help edit mine; I am beyond proud of the woman you are becoming.

To the Ultimate 48 Hour Author team, thank you for making what seemed like an impossible task possible. Natasa Denman, Stuart Denman, Vivienne Mason, Lendy Castillo, Nikola Boskovski, and Hayley Ward, I couldn't have selected a better group of people to work with. Special thanks to Nat for guiding me to choose to invest in myself. You are one amazing lady and leader. Stu, I appreciate your keen insights in making my story come to life and for your kindness and wisdom in calming the noise in my surroundings so I could focus on writing. Nik, your patience with the many revisions to get my book cover exactly perfect. Viv, your kind words of encouragement from the initial half-day retreat to the end of the book kept me believing.

To my friends Michael North, Kenny Bernas, Raquel Rivera, Kat Devera, Abe Anaya, Dr. Jeff Nelson, Amber Rose

Washington, Richard Inez, Christine Rizzo, and Valerie Alviar, thank you for making time to read my manuscript and sharing your heartfelt testimonial.

To my In Loving Arms grief family, this book is ours. Thank you for trusting me, for believing in me, for supporting me, and for your patience as we worked in making this book a reality. Your letters are truly the inspiration of this book.

To our Heavenly Father, thank you for continuing to mold me to be the best version of myself. It's only through you that all things are possible.

> *"We were gonna have a baby, but we had an angel instead." –Pat Schwiebert*

Tani *and* John Leeper

Tani and John Leeper are the authors of **Dear Baby—An Angel We Lost, Love and Honor Forever**, and founders of Jake's Journey Foundation, a non-profit organization providing assistance to the pregnancy loss community.

Trained as an educator, Tani has a unique 18-year background in leadership, communications, and strategic planning. John is an entrepreneur with over 30 years-experience in the marine industry. Driven by his passion and resiliency, he has built a thriving corporation.

For seven years, Tani and John have tirelessly led a support group that empowers parents impacted by pregnancy and infant loss to find their voice while navigating grief. Having suffered two miscarriages and a stillbirth, they know first-hand the monumental heartache and the ultimate gift of finding hope, peace, and their greatest purpose. They have learned that healing comes from taking positive steps over time, openly speaking about grief, and having a clear focus and vison for the future.

An engaging and inspiring powerful duo, they draw from each other through successes and adversities. They offer a relatable message that is an inspiration to others. Tani and John speak on the following topics:

Staying Connected to Your Partner After Loss
- Understanding How Men and Women Grieve
- Busting the Myth that You Can't Have Fun
- Fostering Key Elements Needed in Your Relationship

Finding Happiness and Peace from Tragedy
- Letting Go of the "What Ifs" and "Should Haves"
- Forming Healing Connections
- Finding Blessings in the Ashes

Navigating the First 12 Months
- Understanding Your Emotional Bandwidth
- Discovering Ways to Celebrate the Milestones
- Learning to Ask and Receive from Others

To inquire about enlisting **Tani and John** at your organization or next event, contact them below for rates and availability.

📞 805-285-2313
✉ hello@jakesjourney.org
🌐 www.jakesjourney.org

Notes

Dear Baby

Notes

Dear Baby

Notes

www.ingramcontent.com/pod-product-compliance
Lightning Source LLC
Chambersburg PA
CBHW021148080526
44588CB00008B/256